To Dretz's old friends
with love!

Barry Stucker

Matthew 22:34-40

THE
INSANITY
of
SACRIFICE

THE
INSANITY
of
SACRIFICE

A 90-DAY DEVOTIONAL

NIK RIPKEN

with BARRY STRICKER

PUBLISHING
NASHVILLE, TENNESSEE

978-1-5359-5118-0

Published by B&H Publishing Group
Nashville, Tennessee

Dewey Decimal Classification: 242.5
Subject Heading: SACRIFICE / DEVOTIONAL
LITERATURE / ATONEMENT—CHRISTIANITY

Cover Design by Wideye Design; Roy Roper.
Cover photo cross © nikamata/istock, background
texture © David Methven Schrader/123RF

1 2 3 4 5 6 7 • 23 22 21 20 19

CONTENTS

"My plan will take place, and I will do all my will."
ISAIAH 46:10B

"For my thoughts are not your thoughts, and your ways are not my ways." This is the LORD's declaration.
ISAIAH 55:8

Day 1

What Do You Mean, "Insane"?

"For God loved the world in this way: He gave his one and only Son, so that everyone who believes in him will not perish but have eternal life."

JOHN 3:16

For security purposes I have lived for many years using the pseudonym of Nik Ripken. My wife has used the name Ruth Ripken. We consider it a holy privilege that we have been able to share our story in two previous books, *The Insanity of God* and *The Insanity of Obedience*. The book that you now hold in your hands has grown out of the writing and publication of those previous two books, and it also grows out of our life story.

Before *The Insanity of God* was published, there was serious discussion about the book's title. Many people involved in the debate argued that using the word *insanity* with regard to God would cause people to distance themselves from the book. Some people suggested that the title might even keep the book from being read. That opinion nearly carried the day.

As difficult as it is to gain a hearing in today's world, it seemed that a controversial title might make broad reception of the book unlikely. Sure enough, when the book was published, some booksellers were hesitant even to display the book in public. Sometimes the book was kept behind the counter; at other times, the book was available only by special order.

While the debate about the title was raging, we stood resolute. We fought for the title that was ultimately selected: *The Insanity of God*. Without a shred of disrespect or irreverence, we stressed that God's ways are so unusual that, by human standards, they are considered *outside* of the boundaries of what would be called "sane."

Indeed, God has told us the very same thing in His Word. He is forever reminding us that He is different—and that His ways are different. And not merely different; His ways are scandalous, shocking, startling, disturbing, . . . and holy.

In *The Insanity of God*, we told the story of this unusual God who accomplishes His work in unusual ways. In *The Insanity of Obedience,* we unpacked the lessons of the testimonies and stories of persecuted believers from around the world—and we gleaned from the stories instructive teaching that could assist followers of Jesus seeking to fulfill the Great Commission.

When compared to all the gods recorded in human history, the love and action of Jesus Christ is unusual, mystical, and sacrificial. Whenever did a god allow himself or his son to be crucified for those he created? How could it be possible to envision God sending His Son to die for us as something that is normal, expected, or what we deserve? In other words, is there anything "normal" about God loving us so much that He was willing to make such a great sacrifice?

This *insane* love of God is breathtaking!

And it is this *insane* love of God, introduced in our two previous books, that can take people to unlikely places and cause those people to serve in sacrificial, costly ways.

Indeed, God's way are different.

This God chooses to use people who are not especially qualified. This God chooses to work in ways that we simply do not understand. This God will do whatever is necessary to accomplish His purposes.

This God's love is so out of bounds, so extravagant, so outlandish . . . that we might even call it *insane*.

And this God will allow His children to suffer. This God will ask for great sacrifice. This God will use persecution for His purposes. This God will sometimes leave His children in prison—and He will often leave them there for a long, long time. This God does not always provide immediate rescue; sometimes He does not provide rescue at all. This God loves relentlessly—even when He is rejected. This God even enters into suffering Himself.

The purpose of this devotional book is to help you understand and come to grips with what it might mean for you to sacrifice for the call of Christ. We hope this book will help you hear the expectation of God—and embrace it. God will stop at nothing to accomplish His plan—and He fully expects His people to stop at nothing to give themselves to His purpose.

To help us embrace this crucial task of joining God in His work:

> we will consider the story of God that we encounter in Scripture;
>
> we will learn that God is still very much at work today as we reflect on stories of His miraculous activity around the world;
>
> we will give voice to God's clear demand for obedience that applies to *every person* who follows Jesus.

Ultimately, this exploration will lead us to a point of response—a response that will necessitate sacrifice.

His ways are unusual—so unusual, in fact, that we might even call them *insane*.

Father, forgive us for making You in our image rather than inviting You to transform us into Your image. We want to pray what You taught us to pray: "Your kingdom come, Your will be done, on earth as it is in heaven."

But if we pray that prayer truthfully and sincerely, how much control over our lives will we retain?

Day 2

WE HAVE KNOWN THIS GOD

*No, in all these things we are more than
conquerors through him who loved us.*

ROMANS 8:37

Those who have read *The Insanity of God* or *The Insanity of Obedience* were *reintroduced* to this *insane* love of God. It was not a new introduction to anyone who has already met Him. We have read His story in Scripture. We have encountered His strange ways in history. Clearly, we have known Him, we have walked with Him, and we have loved Him. Perhaps we simply did not recognize just how outlandish God's love is.

One of the central themes of *The Insanity of God* is that the God we read about in the Bible is still at work today—and that He is still doing the very things that He has always done. Our God is not a past tense God!

This also is not an introduction, but a *reintroduction*.

This same God who has been at work from the beginning . . . is at work today, here, now. And this same God is doing the same things He has always done.

It is that great truth that we have discovered through our personal pilgrimage. After a long season of difficult, and seemingly unproductive, ministry in the Horn of Africa—and reeling from the tragic death of our sixteen-year-old-son—we returned to the United States grappling with unanswerable questions. We were close to despair and

5

we sincerely wondered what our next step might be—or even if we had a next step.

Coming out of an environment of debilitating persecution and death in the Horn of Africa, we set out to visit other believers in similar settings to discover for ourselves if Jesus was trustworthy. Is Jesus able to accomplish in the Somalias, the Afghanistans, and the Syrias (and in every other place!) of today what He did among the Roman Empire of His day? Was His resurrection simply an isolated historical event—or is that same resurrection power available to those who walk with this living Jesus today?

Within a brief time, we were given the opportunity to travel the world and learn from brothers and sisters in Christ who had survived—and who were continuing to survive—in settings of severe persecution. Over the next decade, we visited more than seventy-two countries, and interviewed more than six hundred followers of Jesus who live in environments of persecution and the possibility of imminent death. Much to our amazement, we discovered that these fellow followers of Jesus were not merely surviving—they were *thriving* in their faith. And God was blessing them in remarkable and startling ways.

What we learned were life lessons from believers living in persecution, who are living out the resurrection—even today. Our search through seventy-two countries revealed dramatic testimonies of believers who have come to know God intimately as a faithful friend—a friend who calls us to a life of sacrifice modeled after His own.

This matter of sacrifice is a challenge for all of us. And we will be wise to approach any conversation about it with a spirit of humility and prayer. It is our sincere hope that, through the stories contained in these devotions, God will change all of us. It is our prayer that God

will give you a heart for the world. It is our desire that you will embrace
the privilege of sacrificing for His glory.

*God, we are so thankful for Your sacrifice that allows us to
know You as Father, Savior, and Lord. God, we recognize
that You have sacrificed Your Son for us. And we wonder
if maybe that sacrifice should be the end of the story.*

But You invite us to join You in sacrifice.

*Why is our sacrifice still needed? Following You is
so much harder than simply studying about You.
Please give us courage as You call us forward.*

Day 3

JOINING JESUS IN SACRIFICE

"Now go; I am sending you out like lambs among wolves."
LUKE 10:3

✝ God's ways are unusual.

Many of us already knew that. Many of us have experienced God's unusual ways. And we have certainly read about them in the Bible. We might even be able to quote Bible verses that explain or illustrate God's strange ways.

Still, we are startled when we experience God's unusual ways firsthand.

Our typical reaction is one of surprise. *I wouldn't have done it that way,* we might think. Or *I don't understand why God would do that.* God does not normally do what we would do. His ways are different. His sense of timing seems odd. The methods God uses to accomplish His purposes are often very difficult for us to understand.

Nowhere do we see that more clearly than in the central role that sacrifice plays in the activity of God.

We notice first that God's ultimate purpose of redemption is accomplished through the sacrifice of His Son. Beyond that, though, we see that God invites those who walk with Him into a life of sacrifice. Jesus laid down His life for others—and His followers are called to do the same.

If we had only been more careful with our reading of the Bible, we might have noticed it. Perhaps we were paying attention to other themes and patterns. After all, sacrifice is not something we are easily drawn to. But the theme of sacrifice is there on almost every page of both the Old and New Testaments.

> Abram was invited to leave his country, his people, and his father's household (Gen. 12:1). God called him to go to a land that he did not know, and in being sent to this new land, Abram was required to sacrifice all that he had, and all that he knew.

> Some time later, that same man (whose name had been changed to Abraham) was called to sacrifice even his beloved son, Isaac, in obedience to God (Gen. 22:1–19). God graciously intervened and provided an animal that would serve as the sacrifice, but that hard story challenges us to wonder if there is any limit to what God might ask of us.

> In securing a place to build an altar to God, David insisted on paying for the land—even though it was offered to him freely (2 Sam. 24:18–25). David would not consider giving a gift to God that had no personal cost.

> Esther found herself with the opportunity to save her people—at great risk to herself (Esther 4). She approached the king without an invitation, saying, "If I perish, I perish." With Mordecai's help, Esther understood that she was in a unique position, and that she had been prepared "for such a time as this."

> Shadrach, Meshach, and Abednego defied King Nebuchadnezzar's edict and refused to bow before the golden image (Daniel 3). Before being thrown into the

blazing furnace, they declared their trust in God. They knew that God could deliver them if He chose to—but they affirmed their faith in God *whether He rescued them or not.*

When the angel Gabriel visited Mary and told her that she would give birth to Jesus, Mary responded with simple submission. "I am the Lord's servant," she said to the angel. "May it be done to me according to your word" (Luke 1:38). Mary's response is so familiar to most of us that we often fail to see how costly that response would be for her.

Jesus repeatedly called His followers to sacrifice. Those who would follow Him had to enter through a narrow door (Luke 13:24), carry a cross (Luke 14:27), count the cost (Luke 14:28), prioritize His claims above the other claims of life (Luke 9:57–62), and give up everything they had (Luke 14:33).

Furthermore, Jesus celebrated the sacrifice of a widow who gave God everything she had (Luke 21:1–4), and He told a rich ruler to sell everything he had and give it to the poor (Luke 18:18–30).

If we need further evidence of the extent of the required sacrifice, we are told plainly in Ephesians 5:2 to "walk in love, as Christ also loved us and gave himself for us, a sacrificial and fragrant offering to God."

In the New Testament, we meet a follower of Jesus named Paul, a man who embodied a life of sacrifice. Describing his own ministry, Paul noted troubles, hardships, distresses, beatings, imprisonments, riots, hard work, sleepless nights, and hunger (2 Cor. 6:3–10). He wrote to the Corinthians about being hard pressed on every side, perplexed, persecuted, and struck down (2 Cor. 4:7–10). The conclusion is unavoidable: Paul would have had a very different life *if he had not followed Jesus.*

Even so, Paul's various catalogues of personal sacrifices are not complaints. He gloried in the opportunity to suffer for Jesus, desiring only to preach Christ crucified (1 Cor. 1:23), claiming "God's weakness is stronger than human strength" (1 Cor. 1:25), and embracing "the fellowship of his sufferings, being conformed to his death" (Phil. 3:10). Paul actually saw himself as joining in the sacrifice of Christ, explaining to the Christians in Galatia that he had been "crucified with Christ" (Gal. 2:20).

Growing out of his own experiences of sacrifice and suffering, Paul invited others into the same life. He urged the believers in Rome to offer their bodies as "living sacrifices" (Rom. 12:1), and he told the Christians in Philippi that they had been granted the high privilege not only to believe in Christ, but also to suffer for Him (Phil. 1:29).

And we haven't even mentioned John the Baptist or Stephen or Jeremiah. The list of biblical examples and illustrations of sacrifice could go on and on and on . . .

Clearly, sacrifice is a defining theme in the activity of God.

God, we know that sacrifice is central to the story of the Bible. Yet, these stories are old stories; stories in past tense.

God, are You actually suggesting that this kind of sacrifice is something You expect of us? Today?

God, that's terrifying.

How Then Shall We Respond?

Then I heard the voice of the Lord asking: "Who should I send? Who will go for us?" I said: "Here I am. Send me."

Isaiah 6:8

Your first response to the overwhelming biblical emphasis on sacrifice is probably predictable:

But God wouldn't ask that of me. I'm not a character in a Bible story. I'm not a saint. I'm not like Esther or Abraham or Paul. I didn't receive a clear call like Isaiah. God couldn't possibly expect me to live the way those Bible characters lived.

It is one thing to read about God's people in other times and other places who have sacrificed in obedience to God. It is another thing altogether to imagine that God would expect the same of us.

But why would God exempt us from the same sacrifice that He has required from His people throughout history?

God will do anything—ask for anything—demand anything . . . to fulfill His purpose. He even sent His only Son to fulfill His purpose. And when that Son arrived, He declared the purpose of God clearly and openly: "For the Son of Man has come to seek and to save the lost" (Luke 19:10).

That is the purpose of God: to seek and to save the lost, for His glory.

As the people of God, it is both our privilege and our calling to embrace and share in God's purpose. In fact, the very reason for our existence is to join God in His work.

God tells us in Isaiah that the feet that bring good news are "beautiful" (52:7). That concept is developed further, through Paul, in Romans 10:14–15. What is it, exactly, that makes feet beautiful? Feet are beautiful, according to Scripture, when they spread the Good News. In other words, feet are beautiful when they fulfill the purpose for which they were made.

God gave us feet so that we can go and share the Good News!

When we do so, we join God in seeking and saving the lost. We fulfill the purpose for which we were made. We are doing something that, according to God, is truly beautiful.

It is the Great Commission (Matt. 28:18–20) that defines *how*. We go! We go across the street. We go next door. We go down the hall. We go across town. We go across the ocean. And we go so that others will hear about Jesus.

But going will cost us something.

Going will require sacrifice.

What might we be asked to sacrifice?

Almost certainly our time. Maybe our money. We might be required to change our schedule. We will probably be asked to sacrifice our comfort, our safety, and our security. Our sacrifices will certainly affect us, but they will also affect our loved ones. Our sacrifice might affect our physical health, or our life goals.

It could be that we will be asked to sacrifice our very lives.

And if we believe that *God wouldn't possibly ask that of us* . . . we might be very, very mistaken.

God cares so deeply for *every person in this world* that He will do whatever is necessary so that *every person in this world* has the opportunity to encounter His grace.

And God cares so deeply for you and for me that He will not allow us to miss out on being a part of what He is doing.

Amazingly, even the opportunity to sacrifice for the sake of the gospel is an expression of His grace!

Father God, we sometimes believe that if You truly loved us, we would be allowed to die quietly in our sleep at a very old age, after having lived a long, peaceful, and happy life.

We realize today that such a hope lines up with neither Your purposes nor Your promises. We must somehow make room in our lives for the sacrifice that You require, but we are not sure that's what we really want.

Lord, where will this road of sacrifice take us?

Day 5

THE OUTCOME OF DEVOTION

He also appointed twelve, whom he also named apostles,
to be with him, to send them out to preach.

MARK 3:14

It is easy to glamorize or romanticize being sent out. We celebrate people of faith who hear God's call and, on the basis of that call, embrace a life on mission. Incorrectly, we assume that such a call is given to *some* followers of Jesus and withheld from others. And because of that error, we tend to put those who go on a pedestal. We imagine that they have both a higher calling and a greater chance of reaching spiritual heights.

The reality is quite different.

First, this "command" to be on mission is intended for every follower of Jesus. God's call defines *where* we go, not *if* we go.

Second, it is not always glamorous or romantic to be sent.

When we first made our way into Somalia, we were devastated by what we saw. Even worse, we had no training even to absorb and make sense of what we were seeing. Upon our arrival, we were confronted immediately with destruction, poverty, misery, and hunger. We were overwhelmed. We instantly knew that we were ill equipped to survive. And we could not imagine how we might minister in such an environment.

Our prayer during those early days was quite simple: "God, get us out of here!"

We found ourselves in a place that was uncomfortable, strange, and dangerous. It wasn't at all what we had imagined when we thought about being "sent out." If we had known, in fact, exactly where we were headed, we might have put some conditions on our obedience: *Jesus, we will follow You if You take us to a place where we will feel comfortable, settled, and safe.*

When Jesus gathered His group of twelve, He invited them into close fellowship. In gathering this group, Jesus called them close to Himself. But as Mark 3:14 makes clear, He called them close . . . so that they might be sent out.

That same pattern is repeated in the life of every follower of Jesus. Every follower of Jesus is called close . . . so that they might be sent out. Our devotional life, our prayers, our worship, our reflection on Scripture, our growing life of intimacy with Jesus—all of that becomes the foundation for the work that has been prepared for us.

In a word, the outcome of devotion is mission.

As we draw close to Jesus, we begin to see the world the way He sees the world. We begin to care about what He cares about. We begin to love other people the way He loves other people. And we embrace His passion to share His love with every person in the world.

Clearly, going out on mission is no surprise. And it is not a limited calling intended only for some of Jesus' followers. It is, instead, the inevitable outcome of being with Jesus.

We cannot, of course, be certain where exactly He will send us. He sent the disciples out to preach and to drive out demons. He sent my wife and me to Somalia. There is no way to know for sure where He might send you. But wherever He sends you, it will be for the purpose of telling people about Him.

Jesus came "to seek and to save the lost" (Luke 19:10). Then He said, "As the Father has sent me, I also send you" (John 20:21).

Quite simply, we are invited to be with Jesus . . . so that we might be sent out. That dual purpose defines all that we are and all that we do.

Lord Jesus, thank You for calling us close. Thank You for making it possible for us to know You, to love You, and to worship You. We delight in times of devotion. As we spend time with You, we are changed. We understand how important it is for us to be with You.

But can't we be with You without being sent to other people?

Can't we be saved without being sent here, there, and everywhere?

We hesitate to admit it—but we probably already know the answer to our questions.

Day 6

UNQUALIFIED

But I protested, "Oh no, Lord GOD! Look, I don't
know how to speak since I am only a youth."

JEREMIAH 1:6

Ruth and I can vividly recall how we felt when we first
encountered the brutality and suffering of Somalia. We felt
deep despair because we knew intuitively that we had nothing to offer.
Nothing in Somalia looked familiar to us. And little of our education,
training, and experience seemed to have any relationship to the
staggering needs that stood before us.

Those feelings of inadequacy led us to an obvious conclusion: *We*
were completely unqualified for a task that God seemed to be placing in
our hands.

Often people try to keep those feelings of inadequacy private. Even
if we are unqualified in our work situation, for example, we know that
we probably shouldn't admit that openly. We simply carry on and do
our best. All the while, we hope that nobody notices our inadequacy
and insecurity. Even as we put on a good act, it is hard for us to ignore
the secret fear that we carry around. We are certain that we don't know
enough and are afraid that perhaps we'll never figure things out.

That is exactly how we felt when we first arrived in Somalia. And
what a devastating thing to feel.

The good news, however, is that our deep feelings of inadequacy
forced us to lean on God. Like the Prophet Jeremiah, we confessed our

limitations. When Jeremiah heard the call of God, he pointed out to God that "he was only a youth." Jeremiah's response to God made it clear that he didn't have the wisdom or the experience to do what God was asking. But God quickly corrected Jeremiah and explained that God's own presence, wisdom, and power mattered much more than Jeremiah's education or experience.

"Do not be afraid," God said, "for I am with you!"

Jeremiah was not simply being modest or humble. In fact, he was telling the truth. Jeremiah truly was too young and too inexperienced to be qualified for the task. But God made it clear that Jeremiah's response—as true as it might have been—was beside the point. If Scripture tells us anything, it tells us that God tends to call people who are too young, too old, too timid, too inexperienced, or too immoral. God seems to take special delight in calling people who are inadequate for the task and almost certain to fail.

And that is precisely what God had done in calling us to Somalia.

The story is never about the qualifications of the one being called. Rather, the story is always about this bold, risk-taking God who finds the people He wants, and then gives them what they need—so that they might complete the task that He has assigned.

In effect, God says, "I am going to do something here—and I want you to be a part of it. You are, in fact, unqualified. But never forget that I am able."

Bold, risk-taking God, we are inadequate for the task. Our excuses sound perfectly reasonable to us. We cannot imagine why You would want to use us. We are not qualified.

Yet Your command is unmistakable. We hesitate even to pray these words, but we know that You can do more than we ask and more than we can imagine. We know that You can use even us. Through Your power, You can make us adequate for the task. And though our willingness is halting and sometimes tentative, we say . . . Yes.

Use us. Despite our weaknesses, use us.

Day 7

ONE STEP AT A TIME

*The LORD said to Abram: "Go out from your land,
your relatives, and your father's house to the land
that I will show you." So Abram went . . .*

GENESIS 12:1, 4A

✝ Because most of us like to have a plan, we struggle a bit with
God's instructions to Abram (who would later be known as
Abraham). "Go out from your land," God says. "Leave your relatives
and your father's house. Leave all of that . . . and go to the land that
I will show you." God's call to Abraham is simple enough, but it is
remarkably short on details.

Most of us would probably be hoping for something more. In
fact, if we were to hear that kind of command from God, many of us
would ask God for more. We might say in response, "God, thank You
for Your call, but I need additional information. Where exactly will
we be going? How will we get there? Who will pay for this trip? How
long will the journey take? And most important, can You tell me how
things will turn out?"

Abraham's response in Genesis 12 is, however, quite different.
Upon hearing God's unadorned and imprecise call, Abraham simply
obeys.

God says, "Leave," and Abraham leaves.

Later in the New Testament book of Hebrews, we find this assessment of Abraham's response to God:

By faith Abraham, when he was called, obeyed and set out
for a place that he was going to receive as an inheritance.
He went out, even though he did not know where he was
going. (Heb. 11:8)

If we had been watching Abraham at the time, we might have
dismissed his decision simply to leave for an unknown land as foolish-
ness. But today we do not call Abraham irresponsible; instead, we see
him as the epitome of faith and obedience. God told Abraham to do
something that made no sense, something that carried an unspeakably
high cost, something that most people just don't do. And even as all the
follow-up questions swirl in our minds, we read the words that come
next in the story: *so Abraham went.*

We celebrate this story today because it shows us how good it is,
how honorable it is, and how holy it is to believe God so deeply that we
are willing to take one more step . . . even when we have no idea where
that next step might lead.

In this book, we will be reflecting with you on several parts of our
pilgrimage in following God. While God was often very clear with us
when He gave us tasks to do, there were also times when the details
were sparse. We often found ourselves wondering what exactly we were
doing, whether what we were doing made sense, and how things would
work out if we did what God was telling us to do.

Even in those times of uncertainty, God proved Himself to be
faithful. And not one time in our lives have we looked back and
decided that our obedience to God had been a mistake.

Willingness to obey is something God adores. God loved it about
Abraham, and He loves it in His children today.

God is forever on the lookout for people who will take the next
step with Him . . . even when that step makes no sense . . . even when

that next step carries a high cost . . . and even when that next step is something most people just don't do.

If our demand for more details prevents us from obeying God immediately, we may be in danger of missing out on what God has in mind for us.

"Leave," God said to Abraham. "Go. Take a step. I'll show you the next step once you take that first step."

And Abraham left.

God, sometimes we love our plans more than we love You. Sometimes our need for details delays our obedience. Sometimes we will not move forward without assurances and promises and guarantees. Forgive us for making things so complicated.

In truth, all that matters is Your call. Give us the courage to obey. Assure us that the only detail that matters is the certainty of Your presence with us as we go.

Day 8

MAKING THE WORDS OUR OWN

"It is to remain with him, and he is to read from it all the days of his life, so that he may learn to fear the LORD his God, to observe all the words of this instruction, and to do these statutes."

DEUTERONOMY 17:19

In Deuteronomy 17, we encounter specific instructions for the kings who will one day rule Israel. Among other detailed guidelines, each king is expected to write his own copy of God's law, in his own hand. Then, the kings are instructed to read their scroll and to follow faithfully all the words that are there.

This is a remarkable instruction. We might imagine a king saying, in response to this instruction, "Well, I already have a scroll. I can read it anytime I please. So why would I need to write my own copy? That would be a waste of time! Surely, I am too busy to do that!"

But that attitude would miss the point of the instruction. The king was required to write his own scroll because, in the writing of the words in his own hand, the words *become a part of him*. To complete the task of writing, the king would need to slow down enough to allow the words to sink in. And if that were to happen, the king's behavior and character would be affected. In writing these words slowly and carefully, the king would be changed.

It isn't an exact parallel, of course, but in Russia we met a persecuted pastor named Dmitri who knew the importance of allowing Scripture to work its way deep into his heart. Dmitri had been imprisoned for starting an illegal church—something he never intended to do. Early on, he began gathering with his family to read the Bible and sing songs to God. Eventually, his neighbors saw what Dmitri was doing with his family—and they wanted to join in. The group that began to gather eventually grew so large that the authorities noticed. Though Dmitri claimed that he was doing no such thing (at least, not on purpose!), he was imprisoned for starting a church.

He remained in prison for almost two decades. During that time, Dmitri had a habit of gathering small bits of paper that he would find in the prison. On those pieces of paper he would write verses of Scripture that he remembered and the words of praise songs that he had sung in the past. Because he had no Bible, Dmitri could write down only what he remembered. And though he was forbidden to do this, he would stick those Scripture-filled pieces of paper on the wall of his cell as an offering to God.

Somehow, over the years, Scripture had become a part of Dmitri. It had gotten into his heart. Dmitri was not *copying* God's Word—he was, instead, writing all these words *from memory*! The words were so deeply planted in his heart that he could simply call them to mind.

Having God's Word in written form is a treasure and a gift. At some point, however, these written words and these gospel stories need to become a part of our lives. Somehow, we need to plant these words deep in our hearts. Psalm 119:11 invites us to "hide" God's Word in our hearts. When we do that, His words become a vital part of who we are.

For all those years in prison, Dmitri had no written Bible. Even so, he was able to feast on God's Word every day.

God, our lives are filled with so many important things. We have so little time. We are so busy. So You understand, we are sure, why we cannot devote time to Your Word. Simply to read Your Word is often a task that requires so much effort. And to absorb and memorize parts of it? Well, God, that doesn't even seem possible for us. God, remember how busy we are!

But the story of Dmitri gives us pause. Did he somehow have more time than we have? How was he able to make the choice to live daily in the presence of Your Word? We are embarrassed to admit that, if we were in prison with Dmitri, we would not have much to write on our little scraps of paper. Yes, we have access to a written Bible, but we have not always allowed Your Word to grow deep in our hearts.

Lord God, give us a desperate hunger for Your Word.

Day 9

A PEOPLE NOT YET BORN

This will be written for a later generation, and a people who have not yet been created will praise the LORD.

PSALM 102:18

Despite the overwhelming needs that we encountered in Somalia, we were often amazed by the sacrificial service of compassionate people. It seems that, even when the needs were agonizing and the resources were almost nonexistent, there would always be people serving and giving and helping in the most unlikely places.

On one of our first visits to Somalia we went to an orphanage. Within the walls of a small compound, several dozen children received love and care from a few faithful adult workers. There was no electricity and there was no running water. Even though there were no toys, no books, no modern appliances, and no pieces of furniture, the children were cared for in a secure and happy refuge.

Later in the city of Afgoie, we visited a hospital that had been almost totally destroyed by years of civil war. Again, there was no electricity or running water. The only professionally trained staff consisted of a single Russian-trained Somali doctor. Assisted by a few helpers, she worked valiantly to care for dozens of young patients who had been wounded or burned in the fighting.

One tiny child caught our attention. We were told that she was three years old, but she weighed less than fifteen pounds. Shocked at her emaciated appearance and hollow gaze, I (Nik) walked over and simply rubbed one side of her face with my right index finger. Suddenly, she smiled! That smile ruined me. Yet, in that gesture of a simple smile, we were reminded of the human cost of suffering—and we were reminded how often human suffering affects children most profoundly.

Thirty minutes later, that tiny little girl died.

We had no way to make sense of such grievous loss when we first encountered it—and we are not sure exactly how to make sense of it now. But there comes a point when you are so changed by God that your heart simply breaks for the lost and hurting of our world.

At first we embrace the Great Commission because it is a command that has been given to us. Eventually, though, we embrace and obey the Great Commission because our hearts have been broken with the things that break the heart of God.

This question might seem unnecessary, but *why is it important for followers of Jesus to obey His command to go?* Is it enough to go simply because we have been told to go? Certainly, the Great Commission can be read as a command—and there is plenty of motivation in words from Jesus that are a specific instruction for those who follow Him. But ultimately, we go because our hearts are broken from lostness. Ultimately, we go because we have come to love people who are loved by God. Ultimately, we reflect the compassion of God—and that is why we go.

Psalm 102:18 refers to "a later generation" and "a people who have not yet been created." The appeal here is not merely to the children who live today—but to those who will be born in the generations to come. The psalmist has in mind helpless people who desperately need God's grace today—and helpless people in the future who will need God's grace then.

It is important for us to understand that our sacrificial witness today has long-term, ongoing impact. Obviously, our witness today will affect people today. But—as that witness is shared, received, and passed on—it will also affect people not yet born.

Gracious God, overwhelm us with the needs of this broken world. Then overwhelm us with Your power to makes things different.

You are able. You are able to bring wholeness and hope and healing. You are able to save. You look at Your world with deep compassion. You know every name and every need. Help us to look at the world in the same way. Help us to respond to Your call, not merely because it is a command—but also because our hearts break for people created in Your image.

Day 10

THE FAMILY TREE

*God replied to Moses, "I AM WHO I AM. This is what you
are to say to the Israelites: I AM has sent me to you." God also
said to Moses, "Say this to the Israelites: The LORD, the God
of your fathers, the God of Abraham, the God of Isaac, and
the God of Jacob, has sent me to you. This is my name forever;
this is how I am to be remembered in every generation."*

EXODUS 3:14–15

We sat on cushions on the floor. In the middle of the room a feast was displayed on a mat. Though there were only ten of us in the room, there was probably enough food to feed forty people. We had been invited to the home of Ahmed to break the Ramadan fast. During this month-long season of spiritual seeking, Muslims fast from sunrise to sunset each day. They then break the fast each evening with a special meal. Ahmed welcomed us to his home to join him in breaking the fast.

During the meal, we shared our stories. We told Ahmed about our lives and about our faith. He told us about his life and about his faith.

At some point, someone asked Ahmed this question: "Ahmed, how many generations back can you trace your ancestry?"

Many of us can, of course, identify our father and our grandfather and perhaps our great-grandfather. Some of us might do a little better than that. But this young Somali man was able to do significantly better.

He began: "My father is Ibrahim. His father was Ishmael. His father was Mahdi. His father was Omar." *And without even pausing to remember or recall, Ahmed continued for thirteen generations.*

At that point, Ahmed humbly spoke to the group. "I must apologize," he said, "I *should* be able to tell you forty generations, but I confess that I have not thought about this for a long time. I am sorry that I cannot do better."

The lesson we learned that day was not simply that Ahmed had a better memory than we did. Obviously, that was true! The lesson wasn't even that people who live in oral cultures have a better grasp of history than we do. That, too, was clearly true. The real lesson for us was that it is crucial that we understand where we fit in the story—and, specifically, where we fit in God's story.

In Scripture, God is named as the God of Abraham, the God of Isaac, and the God of Jacob. God is known as the God of Sarah, the God of Rebekah, and the God of Rachel. All those names are mentioned not merely because they are part of the ancient history; more than that, those names are all mentioned so that we might see the continuing story and find our place in it. The mention of those names is an invitation. We are being invited to find where we belong—and to remember *that* we belong. We are being invited to remember that God has been at work for a long, long time. We are being invited to think about our family tree—and to think about those people who are our spiritual parents.

God's story didn't start with us. God's story didn't even start with our parents. In fact, God's story started a long, long time ago. And we are a part of what God is doing today because our spiritual parents and grandparents listened long ago to God's call and embraced His purpose and plans.

God of Abraham and Sarah, God of Isaac and Rebekah, God of Jacob and Rachel, remind us of our history and our heritage. Remind us that You have been at work from the beginning. Remind us that faithful people from the past have prepared a path that we can follow.

Lord God, we marvel at the way that You have worked through history. Teach us to learn from the past. Help us to find our place in what You are doing. Allow others to quote our names when they quote their spiritual genealogy.

Day 11

FOCUS

But Jesus said to him, "No one who puts his hand to the plow and looks back is fit for the kingdom of God."
LUKE 9:62

✝ After several dozen trips into and out of Somalia, we were painfully aware of how dangerous our work was. We didn't want to worry our children unnecessarily, but we did want them to understand the nature of what we were doing.

After an especially difficult trip to southern Somalia, we gathered our boys together for a family conference. Shane was thirteen at the time, Timothy was eleven, and Andrew was six.

This is what we told our sons:

*Boys, when we lived in America, even before you were born, we had to answer a very important question: **Were we willing to live our lives for Jesus?** And we decided that we would follow Jesus and live our lives for Him. We decided that we would do that as a couple—and, then, when you all were born, we decided to do that as a family.*

*Later, when we were thinking about being overseas workers, we had to answer another important question: **Were we willing to go with Jesus and live our lives for Him in another part of the world?** We came to Africa after we* *answered that question with another "yes." We came to Africa as a family and, of course, you came with us!*

Now, we are living in Kenya so that we can take food and medicine to help the people who live in Somalia. The reason we're doing this is to show God's love to the Somali people who have never had a chance to know about Jesus and His love for them. But because the Somalis live in a country that is such a hard and dangerous place right now, we have to answer another very difficult question. We have always said that we were willing to live for Jesus. And we decided that we would go for Jesus. We have said "yes" to both of those questions. But now we have to ask ourselves another question: **Are we willing to die for Jesus?**

We didn't want to frighten our sons. We made certain that they knew that we did not expect to die. They knew that we certainly didn't want to die. We assured them that we would take every precaution we could to protect ourselves. But after experiencing the conditions in Somalia, we wanted them to understand the seriousness of the situation. We wanted them to understand how important it was for us to do what we felt Jesus had called our family to do.

Mostly, we wanted them to let Jesus reign. We wanted them to trust Jesus with every detail of their lives.

When we study the Gospel stories of Jesus calling people to follow Him, He is consistent in talking with people about the cost. And He encourages people to count the cost. While there are immense benefits to be gained in following Jesus, there is also a high cost. And Jesus is quite comfortable talking about something that we tend to avoid: the fact that sacrifice will be a central part of following Him.

We fear talking about cost because we suspect that it will keep people from embracing Jesus' call. We fear that people will conclude that following Jesus is too hard or that it will require too much.

In contrast, Jesus holds before people both the benefits and the costs of being His follower—and He then demands that they decide.

God, forgive us for failing to pay attention to the part of the story that focuses on cost and sacrifice. Give us a willing heart so we might trust You even with the sacrifices that will be required of us.

As we share our faith, help us to be honest about the sacrifice that will be required in following Jesus.

HAVING THE RIGHT SPIRIT

Finally, all of you be like-minded and sympathetic, love one another, and be compassionate and humble, not paying back evil for evil or insult for insult but, on the contrary, giving a blessing, since you were called for this, so that you may inherit a blessing.

1 PETER 3:8–9

Over the years, we tried to obey God as faithfully as we could—but we also learned that *how* we obeyed was often just as important as what we did. Sometimes we found ourselves doing exactly what we should have done, but we noticed that our attitude left something to be desired.

While it is surely possible to serve in the presence of suffering with grace and kindness and gentleness, it is also quite possible to serve with an attitude of frustration, bitterness, anger, resentment, unkindness, and impatience. Obviously, we knew that those attitudes were not pleasing to God, but sometimes it was a struggle. It was especially difficult when we were tired and hot and sick.

So much of Scripture is intended to help us become the kind of people God wants us to be. As much as God seeks our obedience—and as important as it is to follow God's laws and guidelines—God's deeper desire is that we become people who will simply reflect His heart and His character. Our ultimate goal is to do God's work . . . and to do God's work in God's way.

In 1 Peter 3, we encounter attitudes and behaviors that are especially fitting for followers of Jesus: unity of spirit, sympathy, love for one another, compassion, humility, and forgiveness. As we served in very difficult situations, we wanted that kind of character to be reflected in our obedience.

Repeatedly, we were blessed with remarkable team members who strived to model that same kind of character. Clearly, we didn't always get it right—given all that we were facing, the challenge of serving with kindness and grace was immense. Even so, it was always our goal for ourselves and for our team members to model the right spirit, to do the things that Christ would do . . . in the way that Christ would do those things.

Obviously, followers of Jesus should seek to do the right things. We should strive to make right decisions. We should desire to provide the right answers.

But more than that, we should strive to have the right spirit.

Our hope is that we will be the kind of people God wants us to be.

Great God, we long to have the right spirit within us. We long for You to have Your way with us so that we might be the kind of people You want us to be. We want to do right things . . . in the right way.

Today, we are not where we want to be. Today, we are not fully the person You want us to be. Today, we do not fully have the right spirit within us.

But we want You to have Your way. Change us. Teach us how to live with sympathy, compassion, humility, forgiveness, kindness, and gentleness. Grow those attitudes in me—and give me a right spirit.

Day 13

TRUSTED WITH A SILENCE

*When Jesus heard it, he said, "This sickness will not end
in death but is for the glory of God, so that the Son of God
may be glorified through it." Now Jesus loved Martha, her
sister, and Lazarus. So when he heard that he was sick,
he stayed two more days in the place where he was.*

JOHN 11:4–6

In John 11 we find the story of Jesus raising Lazarus from the
dead. The first part of the chapter provides the prelude for
Jesus' stunning miracle. In raising Lazarus from the dead, Jesus teaches
us about Himself and He teaches us about His power over even death.
He also demonstrates His deep compassion for the people He loves.

What is perhaps most striking about the story, though, is Jesus'
delay in going to Bethany. In fact, we might find His delay unsettling
and uncomfortable. Jesus is informed of a great need: Lazarus is sick.
We're told that Jesus loved Lazarus, so we can be sure that Jesus cared
about Him. And obviously, Jesus could do something about Lazarus'
need if He chose to.

But after hearing that Lazarus was sick, Jesus *stayed where He was
for two more days.*

Students of the Bible explain that there is a reason for Jesus' delay.
They point out that Jesus knew exactly what He was going to do, that
He had a bigger plan in mind. And that is certainly true. Still, His
delay is hard to understand.

Oswald Chambers in *My Utmost for His Highest* shares this insight about Jesus' delay:

> *Has God trusted you with a silence—a silence that is big in meaning? God's silences are His answers. Think of those days of absolute silence in the home at Bethany! Is there anything analogous to those days in your life? . . . His silence is the sign that He is bringing you into a marvelous understanding of Himself . . . If God has given you a silence, praise Him, for He is bringing you into the great run of His purposes.*[1]

In our lives, there have been many times when God has felt very close. There have been many, many times when God has spoken clearly. But there have also been times in our lives when God has seemed . . . silent. Often, when that happened, we wondered if we had done something wrong. We diligently tried to figure out why God had stopped talking.

It took a long time for us to consider the possibility that God might have been trusting us with a silence.

In some cases, nothing was wrong at all. In fact, we came to understand that the silence was evidence that God was trusting us to carry on with what He had already said to us. And we came to see these times of silence as God's invitation for us simply to watch and wait. In that watching and waiting, we were able to choose to trust God more completely.

Sometimes God speaks very clearly. Sometimes God shows up at the first sign of a need. But sometimes God is quiet. Sometimes God doesn't seem to show up immediately. In those moments, it may be that God is trusting us with a silence.

And when that happens, we should simply carry on, watch and wait. We can be sure that He will act in the right way at exactly the right time . . . no matter what it looks like in the moment.

Lord God, we often assume that You will act on our timetable. Even more, we assume that You should act on our timetable! It's hard for us to wait for You to do what we think You should do. So we pray for patience. We pray for the willingness to watch and wait—and to trust You to do what You desire.

Teach us that Your silence does not suggest Your absence, for we know that You are with us always. You are with us even when we cannot hear You and even when we cannot sense Your presence. Help us to anchor securely to the certainty that, like Lazarus, we too will experience resurrection. You always show up at the right time.

Day 14

THE IDOL OF SAFETY

Those who trust in the LORD are like Mount Zion.
It cannot be shaken; it remains forever.

PSALM 125:1

✝ Many of us are willing to do almost anything . . . as long as we can be sure that we will be safe. Safety, it seems, is one of the core values of our world.

But safety is not one of God's core values. And safety simply cannot be one of the core values of God's people.

In fact, if safety were our main consideration, then safety alone would determine what we would do and where we would go for the sake of the gospel. Our primary question would be: "Is it safe?"

> We would find ourselves sharing our faith *as long as it was safe.*

> We would consider sending out mission teams *as long as it was safe.*

> We would be willing to consider a verbal witness with a neighbor *as long as it was safe.*

> We would make financial decisions as individuals and as churches based on how *safe* those decisions were.

We would find ourselves asking over and over again: "Is this safe?"

One time we heard the leader of our mission sending organization say this: "Clearly, there is a sense in which the danger of our lives increases in proportion to the depth of our relationship with Christ." In other words, *the closer we are to Jesus . . . the more danger we will face in our lives.*

There is, of course, no wisdom at all in seeking danger for the sake of danger. At the same time, however, faithfulness to the commands of God holds more value than safety every time! The people of God are called to faithful response *whether it is safe or not.* If we are faithful, we will go and we will send and we will share and we will speak and we will give and we will pray . . . even when it is not safe.

In our very first interviews in Russia, we heard about pastors and lay people who were imprisoned—and we heard about family members who disappeared into the Soviet Gulag never to be heard from again—because of their willingness to choose faithfulness over safety. These followers of Jesus knew exactly how to avoid these severe punishments; they simply needed to be quiet. They simply needed to hide their friendship with Jesus. They simply needed to stop telling others about Jesus. Had they made those choices, they would have enjoyed safety. But even though it would have been expedient—and far safer—to compromise and withhold witness and deny their faith—these faithful followers of Jesus stood firm at great cost.

Psalm 125 promises a good *ultimate* outcome. But that good ultimate outcome is not immediate. We live in the meantime. And in the meantime . . . there is struggle and cost and, yes, danger.

We live in a time when walking faithfully with God will likely *increase* our suffering!

We live in a time when walking faithfully with God will likely *decrease* our safety!

For the people of God, though, until He returns, it will always be that kind of time. We understand that safety is not our goal.

It probably would have been safer for the children of Israel simply to remain in Egypt. It would have been safer for Moses to remain a shepherd. It would have been safer for Esther not to approach the king. It would have been safer for Shadrach, Meshach, and Abednego to bow down to the idol. It would have been safer for Paul to avoid going to Jerusalem.

And it surely would have been safer for those Russian pastors to not take their faith so seriously.

Even more, it will probably be safer for you to not share your faith with your neighbor. It will be safer for your church to not send out mission teams. It will be safer for you to not get on the plane. It will be safer to not let the world get under our skin. It will be safer to gather for worship each Sunday and simply go through the motions. It will be safer to keep financial resources close to home.

That will all be safer . . . but it will not be faithful.

Safety is not one of God's core values. And it is not a core value for God's people either. Mirroring the character of God, God's people value faithfulness and obedience. And we consider it a holy privilege to do exactly what God has called us to do . . . even if it is not safe.

Almighty God, we are afraid. We live in a frightening time. We are afraid of things that might do us harm. And we are even afraid of trusting You. Most of the time, we would simply like to close the door and stay inside.

Yet, we hear Your call. We cannot ignore it. Give us the courage to walk with You . . . even when we are afraid. Remind us that nothing can separate us from Your love. Set us free from the idol of safety. Do through us what we cannot do in our own power.

Almighty God, be my strength.

Day 15

SHOPPING WITH A PURPOSE

*I have become all things to all people, so that I
may by every possible means save some.*
1 CORINTHIANS 9:22B

✝ We know people who spend extra time in the ethnic food
section of their grocery store; not because they have trouble
deciding what to buy or because it takes them additional time to read
the product. Rather, they spend extra time there because they hope
that they might run into people from other countries who live in their
town. These people have discovered that internationals often purchase
international food—and they hang out in that part of the store hoping
to build friendships with people from other countries.

We know people who return to the same shops over and over
again; not simply because they like the products that are sold there or
because they have been pleased with the customer service. Rather, they
keep going back to the same shops in order to build friendships with
clerks and workers. Yes, these people normally make a purchase when
they visit the shops, but they have a higher purpose in mind. They are
intentionally looking for opportunities for conversation, friendship,
and sharing their faith.

We know people who frequent certain restaurants and choose
to sit in the same section; not because they enjoy the view from their
favorite booth. Rather, they are hoping to have a chance to talk with
the same waiter or waitress. Of course, they eat when they are there,

but their higher goal is to build a friendship. Over time, they are hoping to earn the right to be heard.

We know people who take small packages of food and personal items to the same street corners and alleys week after week; not because those are the only places they could go. Rather, they return to those places so that they can connect with the same people week after week. Many of the people on those street corners are homeless; this is where they live. And people return week after week to share food and personal items—hoping to develop a friendship that might lead to an opportunity for greater ministry down the road.

We know overseas workers who stop in small markets to purchase items *they do not need*. It may look like they are simply absent-minded or that they would benefit from a shopping list. But something else is actually happening. They sincerely hope that those unnecessary purchases will open doors for friendship.

Imagine choosing your check-out line for an evangelistic purpose. Imagine deciding where to purchase gas with missions in mind. Imagine entering into conversations for the expressed purpose of friendship. Imagine intentionally arranging the details of your day in hopes of running into certain people, opening doors for conversation, and building on relational foundations that you've been developing for years.

Of course, most of us don't live that way.

But maybe we should think seriously about why we do what we do.

Perhaps even the simple decisions that we make every day could be motivated by our passion for Jesus—and our passion to share Him as broadly and as often as we can . . .

God, forgive us for compartmentalizing our lives—for believing that each part of our lives has no connection to the other parts. Forgive us for failing to see that our lives—our whole lives—all the parts of our lives—are essentially ways to be on mission. Teach us to open our eyes to opportunities to build friendship and opportunities to share Jesus.

God, we pray for the people we see over and over again. Sometimes that is accidental. Sometimes that is intentional. In either case, show us how to connect with people, how to develop relationships, and how to find ways to share Jesus that are natural and genuine. Help us to love people the way You love people.

Day 16

THE COUNSEL OF GOD

I will bless the LORD who counsels me—even
at night when my thoughts trouble me.

PSALM 16:7

There is a city in West Africa called Touba. It is best known for a huge mosque that stands in the middle of the city. The mosque is the central mosque of the Mouride brotherhood. The building itself is huge, ornate, and impressive. And the crowds that gather at the mosque are immense.

Years ago, a small group of overseas workers traveled to Touba for the specific purpose of praying around that mosque. Attempting not to attract too much attention, the group simply walked around the perimeter of the mosque and prayed for the people who were gathering. After praying, the group found a place to spend the night in a small room at a remote hospital in the bush.

Before going to sleep, the group members reflected on what had happened that day. They shared Scripture and prayed together. One of the group members recited Psalm 16:7 and noted that God often speaks to us in the night, even when we sleep.

The next morning when the group woke up, the man who had shared Psalm 16:7 the night before said that he had a strong impression that the group should return to the mosque at Touba and pray again. That had not been the original plan, but the group eagerly responded to the suggestion. The group returned to the mosque, walked around the perimeter, and prayed.

Nothing at all dramatic happened. There was not a miraculous event. Nothing at all happened that indicated that there was some reason that the group should have returned. On the other hand, we do not always easily or quickly see what God is doing. Perhaps what is most significant is that the group was eager to follow the leadership of God, utterly convinced that God gives guidance, and excited to learn that sometimes God gives us direction even when we sleep.

How good it is to know that God is at work. How good it is to know that God is able to guide us. How good it is to know that God can show us exactly what He wants us to do. We are not left to wonder, to guess, or even to figure things out on our own.

What's more, we even have God's permission to sleep! When we sleep, we place all of our important work in His hands—and we trust Him with that work. It is almost as if every night is a miniature Sabbath. Every night we place our work and our cares in God's hands and we receive His gift of rest.

And, amazingly, sometimes we wake up and we know exactly what to do!

Father, thank You for Your guidance. Thank You
for showing us the way to go. Thank You for the
many ways that You communicate with us.

When You guide us, we long to be obedient. When You give us direction, we delight in following You. Sometimes we understand what You want us to do. Sometimes we do not understand at all. In either case, it is our desire to do exactly what You tell us to do. Help us to obey. Help us to find joy in our obedience.

Day 17

THE PRIVILEGE OF SACRIFICIAL GIVING

During a severe trial brought about by affliction, their
abundant joy and their extreme poverty overflowed in a wealth
of generosity on their part. I can testify that, according to their
ability and even beyond their ability, of their own accord, they
begged us earnestly for the privilege of sharing in the ministry
to the saints, and not just as we had hoped. Instead, they gave
themselves first to the Lord and then to us by God's will.

2 CORINTHIANS 8:2–5

During a time of teaching in a city in Sudan, we were asked if we would be willing to add a new opportunity to our already-full schedule. We happily agreed. For the remainder of that week, we would finish our teaching in the city in the afternoon and then drive out into the bush for evenings of teaching with Muslim Background Believers in a more remote setting.

Each evening, there in the bush, we would simply stop our vehicle under a tree, light a lantern, and wait for believers that might show up. At first, it seemed that no one was even in the area. But quickly, we had a group of about fifteen men and three women.

They were hungry to learn more about the faith. They also seemed especially interested in hearing the stories of persecuted believers in other countries.

As we talked and shared stories, we sensed that the group had something else in mind too. It became clear rather quickly that they were interested in any financial help that we could give them. At that time, there was nothing that we could give them, but we sensed that it was important to follow up on their request.

"Why are you asking us for financial help?" we asked.

Their explanation was simple and to the point: "It is God's will that those who have more should help those who have less."

Keep in mind that we were in a very remote setting. We were literally sitting under a tree in the dark in a desolate area in a nation known for its isolation from the rest of the world.

"Did you all hear about what happened recently in New Orleans in the United States?" we asked the group. "Are you aware of the massive destruction that was caused by Hurricane Katrina? Many people were killed and many other people lost everything. In fact, many of the people suffering there are your brothers and sisters in Christ."

We continued: "Isn't it wonderful that God has sent us here to let you know about their need—so that we can gather a love offering for followers of Jesus in New Orleans who are in such great need?"

We were not attempting to be clever, and we certainly did not want to shame these dear believers in this remote part of Sudan. But we *did* want to help them understand that all who follow Jesus are called to share what they have with one another.

Hearing our words, the immediate response of the group that evening was silence. They were not offended by what we had said, but they certainly were deep in thought.

The next evening when we gathered again under the tree, the group appeared as usual. This time, however, they had a gift that they had brought for the believers in New Orleans. It amounted to about twenty U.S. dollars. We have no idea where the money came from— or how they were able to gather their offering. But they brought it joyfully. They were eager to have a part in helping people who were in need. They were so proud and so happy that they could give.

Writing to the Corinthian church, the apostle Paul holds up the churches of Macedonia as examples for the Christians in Corinth. Even though the churches in Macedonia were small and weak and persecuted, they gave beyond their ability when they learned of the suffering and the need in Jerusalem. We might think that the small and weak and persecuted churches would be exempt from giving—but evidently the Macedonian believers *begged* for the opportunity to give. In this case, the mother church (Jerusalem) was not giving to the mission churches (the churches in Macedonia); instead, the gifts were flowing in the other direction.

In explaining their remarkable generosity, Paul says that they gave "according to their ability and even beyond their ability." He says that "they gave themselves first to the Lord and then to us by God's will."

Somehow, the believers in Sudan reacted to the need of their brothers and sisters in New Orleans in exactly the same way. And they experienced deep joy in their giving.

Gracious and giving God, we cling so tightly to what You have given us. We tend to believe that we have earned all that we have. We tend to believe that we deserve to keep all that we have.

Because of that, we are not always inclined to give it away. Even more, we spend a great deal of time and energy trying to figure out which needs are legitimate and what people might actually do with our gifts and who really does deserve our help.

Forgive us for being selfish with what You have given us so freely. Teach us first to give ourselves to You completely and then to give to those in need. Empower us to give as much as we are able—and then to give even more.

Day 18

LISTENING WELL

*"Therefore take care how you listen. For whoever has, more
will be given to him; and whoever does not have, even
what he thinks he has will be taken away from him."*

LUKE 8:18

✝ One of Jesus' favorite teaching methods involved the use of
parables. His simple, down-to-earth stories were loaded with
spiritual meaning. Those who heard Jesus' parables were sometimes
both enlightened and confused—but there was simply no way to avoid
the power of His words.

In Luke, after using a parable to teach, Jesus explains the meaning of the parable. He then challenges His hearers to . . . listen. Even
more, He challenges His hearers to take care *how* they listen. Jesus is
not merely emphasizing the importance of listening; He is wanting us
to understand that there are ways to listen well.

Jesus' teaching here suggests that understanding leads to even
more understanding. Evidently, there is a way to listen to Jesus that will
allow His truth to sink in, take root, and make a difference. With this
kind of listening, we not only hear the words that Jesus speaks, but we
also embrace those words and act on them.

In our lives, we have always sought to listen carefully to God's call.
From early on, we claimed that we would do anything God told us to
do. And we repeatedly asked God to speak clearly to us. As a matter of

choice and habit, we learned that saying "Yes" to God made it easier and easier to hear His voice.

Because we had already expressed our intention to obey, we found it relatively easy to follow God's guidance when that guidance became clear. Of course, that obedience carried a cost; it normally does. But our decision to respond to God's voice whenever we heard it set us free to obey . . . often without a significant struggle.

In our case, we discovered that we could hear God's voice . . . because we wanted to hear God's voice! And we discovered that we were often able to obey . . . because we had already decided to obey in advance. Jesus' invitation in Luke 8 is not only to listen—but to listen in a way that makes obedience likely.

Educators sometimes talk about "learning readiness." Or we might speak of a "teachable moment." Those ideas suggest that a learner can be in a place where the truth can be received. Obviously, the truth doesn't change. But our willingness to receive the truth—and our willingness to be changed by that truth—does change.

In the same way, God's call is always present. But *how we listen to that call* profoundly influences what we might do in response.

The kind of listening that Jesus calls us to is humble and open. It is listening that indicates a willingness to change. It is an eager and intentional listening. And it is a listening that opens the door for response and obedience.

That kind of listening will likely be a challenge for us. But it is the kind of listening that we will master if we are serious about obeying the call of God.

Speaking God, teach us to listen. More to the point, teach us how to listen in the right way. Teach us how to be eager, hungry, open, and serious in our listening. Teach us that our listening is intended to change us and make us Yours.

After we have learned to listen, give us the courage to act, to answer, to respond. After we have heard You, we pray for the courage to go, to speak, to share, and to love.

Lord God, we want to hear You. Teach us to listen well.

Day 19

DESPERATE FOR PRAYER

"So I say to you, ask, and it will be given to you. Seek, and you will find. Knock, and the door will be opened to you. For everyone who asks receives, and the one who seeks finds, and to the one who knocks, the door will be opened."

LUKE 11:9–10

During one of our extended times of interviewing a large group of house church leaders in China, we were abruptly awakened before dawn one morning by a loud commotion out in the courtyard. We were exhausted from days of interaction, teaching, and sharing with believers in persecution—and we were desperate for sleep. When it was barely daylight, however, we heard loud cries and shouts outside. We immediately thought the security police were raiding our compound. With great concern for the local leaders in attendance, we sheepishly made our way outside to discover our fate.

There were no security police present, however. In fact, what we saw were the house church leaders sitting on the ground in the courtyard with hands lifted and faces turned toward heaven. We couldn't understand their words, but it was obvious that they were pleading with God.

The night before, we had enjoyed a conversation about persecuted believers in other parts of the world. These house church leaders had wondered if people in other parts of the world knew about Jesus. Thrilled to learn that people in other places knew about Jesus, the leaders then wanted to know what life was like for those other believers. As we talked together about believers around the world, we were able to share stories about some of the most severe persecution internationally that had been shared with us. The mood of the group grew somber and serious. That's where we had left things the previous evening.

As we listened to the cries of the house church leaders the next morning, we suddenly began to hear some words that we *could* understand—the names of the places that we had mentioned the night before where the persecution of believers was most severe.

These house church leaders, severely persecuted themselves, had awakened before dawn to pray for believers in other places who were "really persecuted." They had heard about these believers the previous evening. We learned later that they had made a commitment to get up an hour early every morning to pray for these brothers and sisters until Jesus was known throughout those nations and people groups.

Rarely have we experienced that kind of desperation in prayer. Often, in fact, we find excuses not to pray. We believe, for example, that we are too busy. Or that we don't quite know how to pray. Or that prayer is best left to the "religious professionals."

In truth, however, the only reason we do not pray is because we do not believe we need to. Our prayerlessness is often a matter of spiritual pride.

If we sincerely believe that we cannot survive without prayer—if we sincerely believe that others cannot survive without our prayers—we will soon discover a sense of desperation in our praying.

The Chinese house church leaders learned of severe persecution in other parts of the world—and their first response was passionate prayer.

Overwhelmed by the desperate need of others, they simply could not help themselves.

God, we have our reasons. This time it's our reasons for not praying. We are, of course, too busy. We have never really learned to pray— and we are not especially comfortable with prayer. Those are our excuses. Truthfully, though, often we do not pray because we are not really convinced that we need to. We even figure that You have already made a plan and that our prayers will not make a difference.

But You assure us that our prayers make a difference— and that they will make a difference especially to us. In prayer, You tell us, You are mostly trying to change us. In prayer, You are trying to shape our hearts.

And maybe, that is why we really avoid prayer—because we are not always eager to have You shape our hearts!

God, forgive us. Forgive us for thinking that we can make our own way and figure out our own path. Teach us submission. Teach us how to be desperate for You. If You say that we need to pray, then we need to pray. So help us to do just that.

Day 20

IMPERFECT CONDITIONS

*When Jesus heard about it, he withdrew from there
by boat to a remote place to be alone. When the
crowds heard this, they followed him on foot from the
towns. When he went ashore, he saw a large crowd,
had compassion on them, and healed their sick.*

MATTHEW 14:13–14

There are no perfect conditions for ministry and service and mission.

If we wait for the "right" time—when the situation is perfect, when we feel prepared and confident, when everything seems to fall into place—then we likely will never engage in ministry and service and mission. We will, instead, find ourselves waiting for the right time.

During our time in Somalia, the time was never really "right" for ministry. The political situation was chaotic. We never seemed to have all of the necessary resources in place. People were difficult and often unresponsive. Spiritually, we never felt quite ready. But somehow, God made it clear to us that, even so, it was still the "right" time to work and to share and to serve.

This is a good word for all of us. There is always a seemingly good reason not to cross the street and talk with a neighbor. There is always some seemingly good reason why this year is not the year to go on the mission trip—or to learn that new language—or to serve at the soup kitchen. There always seems to be a good reason this isn't the best season to embrace a life of sacrifice for the sake of the gospel.

But if we are not careful, we will miss our opportunities *while we wait for our opportunities.*

In Matthew 14 we read about Jesus' feeding of the five thousand, a beautiful story of compassion and care. But that beautiful story follows hard on one of the most grievous events in the entire New Testament: King Herod has taken the life of John the Baptist. After that hideous event, John's disciples go to Jesus and tell Him what has happened.

And that *seems* to be the end of that particular story—but it is not.

In response to this terrible thing that has happened, Jesus withdraws (by boat) to a solitary place. Clearly, Jesus is grieving and He is deeply burdened. Surely, Jesus deserves some time alone. But the people get wind of His location—and they track Him down. In fact, the people are already there when Jesus' boat reaches land.

These are imperfect conditions for ministry. And in those imperfect conditions . . . Jesus has compassion on the people, and He heals their sick. And then He feeds them.

Given all that has happened, this is not really the best time for ministry. Nevertheless, Jesus provides compassion and healing and feeding and teaching. In these imperfect conditions, Jesus gives Himself.

Some days seem perfect for ministry. But most days are not like that at all.

Some situations seem perfect for ministry. But most situations are not like that at all.

Even so, we are called to go and serve and give and help *every* day—even on the days marked by imperfect conditions. Together, human need and deep compassion come together to provide the ideal conditions for ministry.

Compassionate God, break our hard hearts with the needs of this broken world. Teach us that every moment is the right moment for grace, compassion, kindness, and sacrifice. Set us free from our unrealistic desires for perfect conditions. Teach us that need and compassion are the only necessities for ministry. Show us the deep need of the world. Create in us a heart of compassion. Then, bring together that need and compassion.

Lord God, teach us that this is the right moment.

Day 21

REFINED

For you, God, tested us; you refined us as silver is refined.
PSALM 66:10

Over the years, we have struggled to understand the pain and suffering that fills the world. Before going to Africa, we likely had simple explanations for suffering—but we discovered that our explanations were not adequate to explain the depth of heartache that we encountered.

How do we make sense of suffering? There are really only a few options. Interestingly, all these options are represented in Scripture.

> The first way of making sense of our pain-filled world is to understand that the things that happen in life are the result of human choices and the brokenness of our world. God sometimes is content to let things play out. He is certainly involved, concerned, and connected— but sometimes He does not directly intervene. This explanation suggests that human beings cause many of the hard things that come—things that are hard for themselves and for other people. This explanation makes it clear that some things happen in this world because this world is broken. And that's one way to make sense of our world.

A second way of answering the question is to understand that hard things can be used by God for discipline and correction—and sometimes even punishment. Hard things can sometimes be seen as consequences of sinful behavior. We are told in Scripture that God's discipline is evidence of His love. As difficult as this might be to accept, some hard things that happen in this world might be related to God's discipline or correction. And that is a second way to make sense of things that happen in our world.

A third way of answering the question is to understand that hard things are allowed by God—or perhaps even sent by God—to develop our character. This answer focuses less on the hard things that happen in this world—and focuses more on how God can use those hard things for His purposes. Hard things are sometimes used by God to test us and refine us. And that is yet another way of making sense of our world.

In Psalm 66, the psalmist seems to make a case for this third approach: "For you, God, tested us; you refined us as silver is refined" (v. 10). As simple as that sounds, there is still some question about *why* exactly hard things happen—but there is absolutely no question about what God will do with those hard things. The psalmist believes that hard things can be used to test us—and that God will use those hard things to refine us.

Romans 5:3–4 comes to mind. Adding some thoughts to the actual text, it reads something like this: we also rejoice in our afflictions *(notice that there is no clue or hint here about the source of those afflictions or about whether or not we deserve them)*, because we know that affliction *(wherever it comes from)* produces endurance *(a really good result that can grow from affliction)*, endurance produces proven character *(another really good result that can grow from affliction)*, and proven character produces hope *(yet another good thing—and if we read further in Romans 5, we learn that hope does not ever disappoint)*.

Clearly, God is refining us. If we can be sure of that—if we can truly believe that God is using all that happens to shape us and help us grow—if we can see that God is maturing and purifying us—if we honestly *know* that those good outcomes are happening through hard times—then we will be able to endure whatever might come.

Perhaps it does not matter quite so much where exactly the hard things come from.

Perhaps it is enough to know that God will use those hard things for His purposes.

Lord God, forgive us for thinking that we fully understand Your ways. Forgive us for thinking that we can make sense of this broken world. Forgive us for failing to see Your hand at work in all that happens.

Teach us that You can use anything for Your purposes. Teach us that You can use even suffering, loss, and persecution. Lord God, use whatever is necessary to change us, to shape us, to make us more like You.

Day 22

THE HIGH COST

Then Jesus said to his disciples, "If anyone wants to follow after me, let him deny himself, take up his cross, and follow me. For whoever wants to save his life will lose it, but whoever loses his life because of me will find it. For what will it benefit someone if he gains the whole world yet loses his life? Or what will anyone give in exchange for his life?"

MATTHEW 16:24–26

If we had been giving Jesus advice about His teaching, we might have told Him to downplay the part about the high cost of following Him! After all, Jesus was attempting to enlist followers. He was interested in having more and more people join in His great work. But He talked so much about the cost that many people were hesitant to come along. In an effort to garner a more positive response, we might have told Jesus to talk less about that part of His call.

Jesus, however, never minimized the cost. And He certainly never omitted that part of the story when He called people to follow Him. He was direct and open and honest. He assured people that, along with the unspeakable joy of following Him, there would certainly and unavoidably be suffering and sacrifice. Jesus never hesitated to talk about the cost.

And if we are wise and honest, we too will choose to talk openly about the high cost of following Jesus. We will follow His example and make the cross a central part of our message.

Over the years, many people have been deeply affected by a book that emphasizes that very point. Entire generations of believers have been moved and changed by Dietrich Bonhoeffer's *The Cost of Discipleship*. Reading the book, it's so easy to say to your closest friends, "You've got to read this! It changed my life!"

Bonhoeffer's words challenge the comfortable and convenient life that many people seem to seek. Very much in line with the teachings of Jesus Himself, Bonhoeffer claims that sacrificial suffering is not some terrible surprise that meets us on the journey—nor some tragic mistake that shows up without warning—but quite simply the natural and expected outcome of following Jesus.

In his words:

> The cross is not the terrible end to an otherwise God-fearing and happy life, but it meets us at the beginning of our communion with Christ. When Christ calls a man, he bids him come and die.[2]

What a staggering thought . . . that we are called first to the cross . . . and that following Jesus means leaving everything else behind.

Obviously, these are not easy words. And obviously, this is not a lesson that we have mastered. But Jesus' call is clear. And He still speaks those same words to those who would be His followers today. Jesus still seeks followers who will take up the cross.

Sacrifice is not merely the sad lot of some few believers who happen to live in tough places. Instead, sacrifice is the life of any and all who would follow Jesus.

The cost of discipleship is high. Jesus has always been completely open about that. He makes the certainty of sacrifice clear from the very beginning.

It is no wonder that so many walk away from Him.

But where, exactly, would we go? After all, He alone has the words of eternal life!

Lord Jesus, this is a hard word. We would much rather focus on the joy of walking with You. We would much rather hear about the blessings and the benefits. And, yes, those joys, blessings, and benefits are immense!

But, still, there is that cost. And You place that cost before us when You first encounter us. Clearly, You want us to understand all that it means to follow You.

Empower us to embrace this high cost. Give us the courage to lay everything down so we might follow You. Teach us over and over again that You are worth even the highest cost.

Day 23

JONAH, JOB, AND JESUS

*The Spirit himself testifies together with our spirit that
we are God's children, and if children, also heirs—heirs
of God and coheirs with Christ—if indeed we suffer
with him so that we may also be glorified with him.*

ROMANS 8:16–17

✝ Let's talk a little more about suffering.

Reflecting on our lives—and preparing this book—has caused us to think a great deal about suffering. One of the things we keep thinking about is why exactly suffering happens.

Three Bible characters come to mind. Their stories are complex and textured. At the most basic level, though, all three of these characters have something important to contribute to our understanding of suffering.

First, there was Job. Job suffered profoundly and, according to Scripture, suffered through no fault of his own. Even further, Job seemed to have been singled out for suffering *because* he was righteous and blameless. Though Job's friends insisted that he had done something to deserve his disasters, Job resolutely defended his character and his heart. He was ultimately brought to his knees before God, but God never suggested that Job was responsible for the suffering that came his way.

So that is our first possibility: sometimes suffering simply happens. Perhaps it comes because this is a fallen world. Perhaps the actual reason for suffering is beyond our understanding. Perhaps God has purposes in suffering that we cannot easily grasp. Perhaps other people are responsible for our suffering. In any case, this kind of suffering comes and it is not specifically our fault. Suffering simply happens.

Second, there was Jonah. Jonah suffered too. But unlike Job, Jonah's suffering was the result of his own choices. Jonah's disobedience led to costly pain in his own life—and in the lives of others as well. Jonah's suffering was different than Job's suffering. Jonah's suffering was specifically caused by his own sin, his own disobedience, and his own refusal to follow God.

That is our second possibility: sometimes suffering comes directly or indirectly from our own choices. Those choices might be intentional or simply careless, but this kind of suffering reminds us that our decisions and actions have consequences for ourselves and for others.

Third, there was Jesus. Jesus' suffering is incomparable. What is most remarkable about Jesus' suffering is not only that He freely chose it, but that it was the result of doing what was right. Jesus followed the call of His Father—and His obedience led to immense suffering. This was the exact opposite of Jonah's experience: suffering not because of sin, but suffering tied directly to obedience.

That is our third possibility: suffering caused by righteous, God-honoring choices. We can see other examples of that kind of suffering in the Bible—Daniel, Paul, and Stephen come quickly to mind—but Jesus is the supreme example.

So why, exactly, does suffering come to us?

It could be that our suffering is simply something that happens in a broken, fallen world. In some cases, what happened to Job may happen to us.

It could be that our suffering is a result of our bad choices. In some cases, what happened to Jonah may happen to us.

And it could be that our suffering is the result of our faithful obedience to God. In some cases, what happened to Jesus may happen to us.

Every believer in persecution that we have interviewed has suffered; some have suffering grievously. In almost every case, as far as we can tell, their suffering has been the inevitable outcome of a faithful, obedient response to the call of God. If that is truly the cause of our suffering, we can embrace it joyfully—because that kind of suffering is a godly and noble thing.

Lord God, there is so much that we do not understand. We struggle to make sense of suffering. Even though we know better, we want to believe that our faithfulness will lead only to good things. And, ultimately, faithfulness DOES lead to good things! But in the meantime, faithfulness can lead to imprisonment, loss of family, torture, ridicule, pressure, and even death. We have learned from persecuted followers of Jesus that faithfulness almost certainly leads to suffering.

Help us to trust You in times of suffering. Help us to minimize those situations where our poor choices lead to suffering. In other situations, give us the courage to be faithful even if suffering is the result. To use the words of the apostle Paul, help us to be willing to suffer with Jesus.

Day 24

CALLED

*The LORD came, stood there, and called as
before, "Samuel! Samuel!" Samuel responded,
"Speak, for your servant is listening."*

1 SAMUEL 3:10

One of the core convictions of our faith is that God speaks.
Even when we don't know exactly what to do, we are not
left on our own. God has promised to provide us with direction and
guidance and leadership. God may speak through the Bible or through
prayer or through trusted friends or even through circumstances.

However He chooses to speak, though, we can be certain that
God speaks.

From the very beginning, God makes clear His desire for friendship—so a relationship with God is central as we come to faith.
Following that, God continues to guide us and show us the way to
go. Throughout our lives we have stood at crossroads, holding in our
hearts multiple options, weighing the wisdom of different choices—
and God has always been clear in providing direction.

When we first went to the mission field as a young couple, we
asked God for wisdom in developing a ministry in Malawi. When it
became clear that we could not remain in Malawi because of malaria,
God led us clearly to the Transkei in South Africa. As we ministered
there, we reread the book of Acts and God directed us to the Horn of
Africa where we could minister among the Somali people. After my son

Tim's death, God tenderly led us home for a season of healing—and then He opened doors so that we could travel the world to learn from the persecuted church. As we journeyed from country to country, God brought us to the right people and sent us to the right places so that we might hear the stories that He wanted us to hear.

Sometimes, we are inclined to believe that, even as we cross the street or cross the ocean to fulfill our calling, it's up to us to figure things out. But God guides our steps as we obey.

> How often have you seen God arrange a personal encounter or shape circumstances in a way that would make witness possible and productive?

Young Samuel experienced the voice of God—and he needed help discerning what God was saying. In fact, he needed help even discerning that it was God who was speaking! In response to Eli's good counsel, Samuel opened himself to the voice of God. The words that Eli gave Samuel to speak are words that we should all copy in our walk with God: "Speak, for your servant is listening." Hearing, "Nik, are you ready to follow Me?" in that factory so many years ago is consistent with a God who speaks.

What happened to Samuel happens between God and ourselves. With great fanfare—or with no fanfare at all—God speaks today. For many He speaks through His Word, the Bible. He speaks to call us into friendship. He speaks to give us direction. He speaks and tells us about things to come. He speaks to correct and discipline. He speaks to assure us of His love. He speaks and sends us out on mission.

And all of that speaking is clear and unmistakable and impossible to ignore.

Once we hear God speak, we decide what exactly we will do in response to what He has said.

God does speak. We can hear Him if we choose to.

And once we hear Him, like Samuel, we have decisions to make.

Speak to me, O God.

We long to hear Your voice. Even before we know exactly what You will say, our answer is clear and unequivocal. We say: "Yes!"

Teach us to be still enough to listen. Give us sensitive ears and open hearts. Your Word will guide our lives and shape our living.

Day 25

NOT COMPETENT

"My God, my God, why have you abandoned me?"
MATTHEW 27:46B

✝ In August of 1992, the United States committed ten military cargo planes to airlift United Nations relief aid into Somalia. In the next five months, those planes delivered almost half a million tons of food and medical supplies in Operation Provide Relief.

Still, nothing changed much in Somalia during 1992. Violence and anarchy still reigned in a country where the death toll by starvation surpassed five hundred thousand. Another 1,500,000 people had become displaced refugees. As much as 90 percent of the supplies now pouring into the country continued to be looted by one clan. Much of what was not stolen was store-housed in airport hangars. The United Nations didn't have the organizational resources to deliver the aid into the hands of the people who most desperately needed it nor protect it from General Caydiid's (Aydiid's) militia.

During that time, we provided mobile medical clinics outside the city of Mogadishu. We also intensified our effort to establish and service five feeding centers in and around Mogadishu. Our teams distributed food for ten thousand people each day at each center. That meant that, beginning in 1993, we were able to keep fifty thousand people a day from starving. In addition, we continued to provide medical relief, offer basic survival resources, and resettle displaced families.

Most of the people we helped were internal refugees who had flooded into the city from the countryside because of drought, civil war, and famine. They had no jobs, no money, and no resources. They slept in abandoned buildings, makeshift tents, and hodgepodge shelters.

When our teams first arrived in the distribution locations, people often asked if we had any white muslin cloth. We could not make sense of the request until we were told that bodies were required to be ceremonially wrapped in white cloth for proper Islamic burial on the day of death. We then understood that people were asking for white cloth so that they might bury their children and relatives who had died during the night. Once that responsibility was fulfilled, the people could deal with their other needs.

We quickly learned that, wherever we went, we needed to have not only food and water, but also bolts of white cotton cloth.

While we were gratified to be able to help, we were overwhelmed with the suffering and need. No matter what we felt we had to offer, we knew that it was not enough. We were not big enough or strong enough or good enough for a task of this magnitude. And while we had excellent Western-based theological and missiological training—and while we had massive amounts of food and medicine—we were not equipped for the horrific needs that stood before us.

The root of Somalia's grievous struggle was not based in famine or civil war. Somalia was under attack by evil.

How does our dressed-up, building-based, Western Christianity oppose such evil? Where should we have gone and who should have prepared us to battle such evil? We were aware that we had been sent out as "sheep among wolves." Yet to be untrained for this intense spiritual warfare—almost "foolish sheep"—was unacceptable!

Added to this devastation throughout Somalia, the few believers in Jesus were being hunted down and martyred. Four of our best Somali friends were killed on one day . . . in a forty-five-minute period. We sincerely did not know how to serve God in settings like these. We struggled daily with what it meant to be New Testament followers of Jesus, serving in an Old Testament environment.

We knew that we were simply not competent for such a task.

Over time, we came to understand that God alone was competent to address this level of need. Even though we were committed to the task, we were broken and overwhelmed. In our desperation, we were driven to trust God more and more completely.

In that trust, we discovered the incomparable competence of God.

*God, sometimes sacrificing our time, our talents,
and our safety for the sake of others is met with more
demand, greater need, and less security.*

*Lord, how can You possibly ask us to leave our New Testament
world and serve in an Old Testament environment? We thought
that simple inconvenience was a difficult sacrifice. But now
we are beginning to understand the extent of Your call.*

*Give us courage to go. Teach us that when we
are not competent, You are able.*

Day 26

THE REALITY OF EVIL

*Finally, be strengthened by the Lord and by his vast
strength. Put on the full armor of God so that you can
stand against the schemes of the devil. For our struggle
is not against flesh and blood, but against the rulers,
against the authorities, against the cosmic powers of this
darkness, against evil, spiritual forces in the heavens.*

EPHESIANS 6:10–12

Scripture tells us the truth about God. From the Bible,
we learn that God is love. We also learn that God desires
friendship with human beings and that He has made a way for that
friendship to happen.

Scripture also tells us the truth about evil. From the Bible, we learn
that there are forces at work that oppose the activity and purposes of
God.

The apostle Paul emphasizes the spiritual nature of those oppos-
ing forces. He explains that "our struggle is not against flesh and
blood, but against the rulers, against the authorities, against the cosmic powers of this darkness, against evil, spiritual forces in the heavens" (Eph. 6:12). While our struggle is not against flesh and blood,
Paul is realistic enough to understand that those spiritual forces of evil
are often made manifest in flesh and blood. Clearly, spiritual forces
were working against Paul as he passionately pursued God's call in his

life—but there were also very real people who put him in jail, threw rocks at him, and ran him out of town.

Paul understood the Lord's instruction about loving enemies, but he never denied the existence of those enemies. Even more, he was wise as he dealt with those who sought to do him harm. And part of his wisdom was acknowledging that evil was real—and that evil sometimes showed up in the behavior and attitudes of people who were opposed to God.

Persecuted followers of Jesus have told us often that they prayed for their persecutors. Specifically, they prayed that their persecutors would come to know Jesus. In fact, they pointed out that the best way to deal with persecution was to turn your enemy into a brother or sister in Christ.

At the same time, we cannot recall a single interview where the evil of the persecutors was dismissed or discounted or minimized. Instead, we heard story after story of unspeakable mistreatment—actions that were intended to destroy both the faithful servants of God and the gospel itself. Persecution, we learned, is not simply disagreement about religious matters—it is, instead, an intentional effort to destroy God's people and thwart the purposes of God.

The ultimate goal of persecution is to keep people from Jesus. And persecutors will do whatever is necessary to reach that goal. Through years of interviews, we heard stories of all manner of persecution (ranging from rather mild intimidation all the way to execution—and just about everything in between). At first, we thought that, surely, nothing could be worse than death. But then we heard stories about severe and unspeakable efforts of persecution that caused us to question our initial assumption. Perhaps some of the suffering that we heard about was, indeed, worse than death!

In Somalia, we saw believers murdered because they were believers. In East Asia, we heard stories of unspeakable physical brutality and psychological torture. In Egypt, we learned that persecutors often left Christian pastors alone—instead focusing specifically on destroying the families of those pastors. In particular, the teen-aged daughters of pastors in Egypt were targeted. These daughters were enticed and even forced into marriages with Muslim men specifically to invalidate and discredit the ministries of the pastors who were their fathers.

We certainly believe that God's power is greater than any evil that can come against God. At the same time, we are wise to understand that any follower of Jesus who determines to be faithful and bold in witness will be attacked. And those attacks might come in many different ways—and often those attacks might come in unexpected ways.

Jesus sent His followers out "as sheep among wolves" (Matt. 10:16). Jesus sends us out today "as sheep among wolves." Given that reality, he counsels us to be shrewd (Matt. 10:16).

Evil is real. There are forces in our world—and forces beyond our world—that oppose the activity of God. If we are faithful to God's call, those forces will oppose us.

But God is strong and God is trustworthy and God will ultimately have His way.

Frankly, God, we are uncomfortable with this part of the conversation. We realize, of course, that evil exists. But we tend to deal with evil at a theoretical level. It gets uncomfortable when we talk about real people doing actual evil things—in an effort to oppose Your purposes. We don't have a way to make sense of that.

It's hard enough for us to be bold in witness when everybody is cheering us on. How in the world are we going to be bold when we face hate-filled opposition?

We hear the stories of those who are much more acquainted with evil than we are, and we are shaken to the core. We fear that we do not have the courage for this kind of warfare. So we need Your help. Teach us how to stand firm. Teach us how to be faithful. Teach us how to be true to Your call. Teach us how to suffer for You. Teach us wise actions. Teach us that You are stronger and greater than evil.

Day 27

WASTED YEARS

After a long time, the king of Egypt died. The Israelites groaned
because of their difficult labor; and they cried out; and their
cry for help because of the difficult labor ascended to God.
And God heard their groaning; and God remembered his
covenant with Abraham, with Isaac, and with Jacob; and
God saw the Israelites; and God knew. Meanwhile, Moses
was shepherding the flock of his father-in-law Jethro . . .

EXODUS 2:23—3:1A

After so many years serving in Africa, we were left wondering what, if anything, we had accomplished. Certainly, we had experienced wonderful seasons of ministry in both Malawi and Transkei. But years of what seemed to be fruitless work in the Horn of Africa forced us to rethink even those earlier times.

Even though we had worked hard and even though we had done our best to be obedient to God's call, there was almost nothing to celebrate. We desperately wanted to share Jesus with our friends and coworkers, but we also knew that our sharing with them could very well lead to severe suffering and persecution in their lives. And if, by God's grace, someone actually responded to our sharing and made the personal decision to follow Jesus, we were aware that their wonderful decision could lead to their death.

We certainly felt the awesome responsibility to share Jesus—but we also knew that we had to find ways to do that wisely and strategically.

Though we tried hard to do just that, we were not often successful. After years, we could not identify much fruit that had been produced.

In fact, from a human point of view, things got worse and worse the longer we stayed in Somalia. Not only were we not seeing measurable fruit; even worse, our presence there seemed to be doing damage to the cause of Christ!

All the while, we wondered what God was doing. Despite our obedience—and despite what we considered to be our sacrificial service—those years in Somalia often felt like wasted years.

We should have known better, of course. We should have known that God wastes nothing. At the time, however, we wondered.

In his recounting of God's activity, Stephen in Acts 7:23 said that Moses was forty years old when he left Egypt and arrived in the wilderness. Exodus 7:7 makes it clear that Moses was eighty years old when he returned to Egypt. Working with that time line, we understand that forty years passed between the time Moses left Egypt and the time that he returned to Egypt. Forty years is a long time—so long, in fact, that it would be easy for us to describe those forty years in the middle of Moses' life as *wasted years*.

Forty years is a long time to take care of sheep in the wilderness! And as far as Moses knew at the time, taking care of sheep in the wilderness was all there would ever be for him.

But God knew far more than Moses. And eventually, Moses would come to understand that those forty years were not wasted at all. In fact, those forty years were Moses' preparation for heroic, God-honoring work. Unseen, God was working that entire time.

We tend to talk about interruptions, detours, delays—and even wasted time. But God has a different perspective. Every time is His time. Every place is His place. And even the years that we might call "wasted" are being used for His purposes.

For our part, God was using "wasted years" to teach us more and more about His unusual ways, about His heart for the world, about His relentless commitment to keep His promises, and about how important it was for us to become the kind of people who could be most useful to Him.

Though we could point to so little, we came to understand that God was working every day—even during all those so-called *wasted* years.

Holy God, we are impatient. We loathe waiting. We especially hate to wait when we cannot see anything happening. When we feel that way, forgive us for our focus on darkness instead of the Light. Teach us to slow down—and to believe deeply that You are at work—even when we cannot see what You are doing. Holy God, do what You desire to do in Your time.

We will find it a struggle, to be sure, but we will take care of sheep for forty years in the wilderness if that is part of Your plan. As we do that, we will stubbornly believe that You are at work even there. Teach us to trust You, and give us eyes to see.

Day 28

His Cross . . . and Ours

Now great crowds were traveling with him. So he turned and said to them: "If anyone comes to me and does not hate his own father and mother, wife and children, brothers and sisters—yes, even his own life—he cannot be my disciple. Whoever does not bear his own cross and come after me cannot be my disciple."

Luke 14:25–27

We are not sure where exactly we picked it up, but somewhere along the line it became part of our life outlook; the idea that obedience to God's call would result in a life of safety, security, and success. As far as we can remember, nobody ever said that out loud, but somehow it just seemed to make sense. And it simply became part of our understanding of how the world works.

> *If you do what God calls you to do—and if you give your best and trust in Him—and especially if you sacrifice in your service—God will bless you with both safety and success. If you pray regularly, work hard, have the needed resources, and the right people working together, success is guaranteed.*

We knew better than to actually believe such things, of course, but it is funny how incorrect and misleading ideas can creep into our minds and hearts—and how those ideas can begin to shape our view of God and His ways.

Over the years, we devoted ourselves to what we considered sacrificial service. Instead of safety and success, we experienced significant loss, heartache, and failure. We saw people come to faith in Jesus—and then we watched as those people died for their faith. We expended immense time and energy in service—and we could point to almost no good result that could be measured or quantified. We tried our best to live faithfully—and we experienced deep tragedy in our personal lives.

And we weren't the only ones with this experience.

In our conversations with hundreds of brothers and sisters in persecution around the world, we have heard stories with similar outcomes. Their embrace of sacrificial suffering was never in question. They lived with great faith and devotion. They obeyed God. They loved God profoundly. But the outcome of their good and godly living was neither safety nor success. Instead, there was persecution and suffering and loss. There was pain and heartache.

The *ultimate* outcome, of course, was something quite different. In our lives and in the lives of these persecuted brothers and sisters, God transformed all that suffering and pain into something grand and glorious—and we should never doubt God's ability to do that sort of thing.

But what surprises us is what happened in the short term. What surprises us even more is God's eager willingness to use painful sacrifice to accomplish His purpose.

Long ago, after Peter boldly declared that Jesus was "the Messiah, the Son of the living God" (Matt. 16:16), Jesus immediately launched into a conversation about sacrifice.

First, Jesus talked about His own sacrifice—what would happen to Him and what He would suffer. But then Jesus talked about the sacrifice that would be required for those who would be His followers.

For Jesus, obedience would carry a high cost. For Peter and his companions, obedience would carry a high cost. And for those who follow Jesus—even today—obedience will carry a high cost.

We enjoy stories with happy endings. We enjoy stories about people who live with great faith—and people who enjoy the fruit of great faith. We enjoy stories where things work out, stories where God shows up, and stories where there is a dramatic rescue in the nick of time.

And, praise God, sometimes that happens.

But sometimes, at least in the short term, happy endings are hard to find. Sometimes things don't seem to work out—and sometimes God seems strangely silent. Sometimes there is no dramatic rescue in the nick of time.

Even then, we trust God to work and move.

Even then, we trust God to redeem even our failure.

Even then, we wait to see what God will do.

And while we wait, we embrace the sacrifice that is central to His call. While we wait, we invite God to use our sacrifice any way that He desires.

Lord God, forgive us for expecting certain outcomes as we walk with You. Teach us to submit to Your unusual ways. Draw us to a life of joyful obedience—and remind us that our obedience will necessarily require sacrifice.

Father, we deny ourselves.

We take up our cross.

We eagerly follow Jesus.

Day 29

FOUNDATIONS

*Remembering your tears, I long to see you so that I may
be filled with joy. I recall your sincere faith that first
lived in your grandmother Lois and in your mother
Eunice and now, I am convinced, is in you also.*

2 TIMOTHY 1:4–5

As we think about God's command to go, we would be wise also to revisit the very beginnings of our relationship with Jesus. Every follower of Jesus has a unique and personal story. The common strain in every story, though, is that *somehow* God found a way to reach us. Beyond that, our individual stories are diverse and different.

For some of us, our conversion seemed as simple as taking the next step. Embracing Jesus as Lord and Savior happened naturally and without much drama. For others, we came into the kingdom kicking and screaming. In some cases, conversion is very dramatic. Some of us might note that our early spiritual steps were marked by fits and starts.

In Ruth's case, entering into friendship with Jesus was a natural next step that grew out of a spiritual heritage that she knew from birth. In my (Nik's) case, there was a powerful encounter with God in a worship service that focused on the resurrection of Jesus—but then years of disinterest that followed that worship service. Eventually, God would draw me close—but that would take a more dramatic encounter with God.

How exactly salvation "happens" is not always easy to determine. But somehow God has a way of reaching us—and He is very patient as He works to draw us close.

The apostle Paul encourages young Timothy to remember his spiritual foundation. In his letter to Timothy, Paul mentions Lois and Eunice, Timothy's grandmother and mother. Paul calls to mind the faith that lived first in them. He then says clearly that the same faith now lives in Timothy. The faith has been passed down, and Timothy is a recipient of a precious heritage.

Repeatedly, we encountered the same story in our conversations with persecuted followers of Jesus around the globe. These deeply committed followers of Jesus, in every case, had been nurtured by someone. Someone had introduced them to Jesus. Someone had taught them and nurtured them and helped them grow. And in most cases, someone had taught them how to suffer for the sake of the gospel.

That same passing-down-of-the-faith has happened to every follower of Jesus.

It is a wonder that God finds a way to reach us. His grace, however, carries with it a great responsibility. We have been brought into friendship with God for a reason. We have heard the story of Jesus so that we might share it with others.

Perhaps the names are different in your story, but there is probably a "Eunice" and a "Lois" in your spiritual ancestry. Among unreached peoples, where there is no "Lois" or "Eunice," no believing "Abdullah" or "Fatima," then the "Niks" and "Ruths" must stand in the gap.

Who first told you the stories of Jesus? Who helped you understand God's heart for the world? Who encouraged you to grow? Who picked you up when you failed? Who loved you into the kingdom? Who passed on the faith to you?

We have been entrusted with a precious gift. And now it is our responsibility—and it is our privilege—to "keep ablaze the gift of God" (2 Tim. 1:6 HCSB).

Gracious God, thank You for finding us, for reaching us, for saving us. Thank You for the people in our lives who helped that happen. Thank You for the people who played the role of "Eunice" and "Lois." Thank You for the faith that first lived in them—and thank You for the faith that, because of them, now lives in us.

Help us to honor our spiritual foundation by keeping ablaze the gift of God that we have been given.

Day 30

AN UNDIVIDED HEART

*"I will give them integrity of heart and put a new spirit
within them; I will remove their heart of stone from their
bodies and give them a heart of flesh, so that they may
follow my statutes, keep my ordinances, and practice them.
They will be my people, and I will be their God."*

EZEKIEL 11:19–20

As we grew in our friendship with Jesus, we confess that we were often a little naïve. We saw no need to complicate instructions of Scripture that seemed utterly clear. When we read the Great Commission (Matt. 28:16–20), for example, we simply concluded that those words applied to us. We *knew* that those words applied to us, because they clearly applied to *every* follower of Jesus. We saw those important words of Jesus not as a suggestion or as a possibility or as an idea to consider—**but as an absolute command**. We had claimed Jesus as Lord, and we simply believed that it was essential to obey what our Lord was telling us to do.

To be sure, we did not always understand exactly *how* we could fulfill Jesus' commands, but we simply assumed that obedience was possible—because we knew that Jesus wouldn't command us to do something that could not be obeyed. Again, we did not always get it right—and we made plenty of mistakes—but we tried out best to respond to Jesus' commands with quick and trusting obedience. As much as we were able, we wanted our hearts to be completely

His—and we knew that our obedience would illustrate our sincere desire to be as committed as possible.

Long ago, God spoke a word of judgment to the leaders of Israel through the prophet Ezekiel. God explained that leaders have a special responsibility, and He called these particular leaders to account for their unfaithfulness. It was a fairly severe word of judgment.

Following that word of judgment, though, God spoke a tender word of hope and restoration. Through Ezekiel, God said, "I will give them integrity of heart and put a new spirit within them; I will remove their heart of stone from their bodies and give them a heart of flesh" (Ezek. 11:19).

Through the prophet Jeremiah, God said something very similar: "I will give them a heart to know me, that I am the LORD. They will be my people, and I will be their God because they will return to me with all their heart" (Jer. 24:7). The psalmist, too, prayed: "Teach me your way, LORD, and I will live by your truth. Give me an undivided mind to fear your name" (Ps. 86:11).

God desires that we have an undivided heart—and radical obedience is evidence of that kind of heart.

According to Scripture, the human heart is the seat of the will. The heart is where decisions are made and where the course of action is determined. To have an undivided heart is to understand clearly what God desires *and* to act on what God desires. When we live that way, our hearts are alive, shaped by God, sensitive, and in tune with Him. When we live that way, our hearts are truly undivided.

When it comes to the commands of Jesus, it is good to be naïve. It is good to understand that His commands *are* commands. And it is good to understand that those commands apply even to us.

Loving God, we belong to You. Do in us what You alone can do. Do with us what You alone can do. Take our cold, hard hearts, and replace them with hearts that are alive, sensitive, and responsive. Give us undivided hearts—hearts that hunger for You, hearts that care about what You care about, hearts that break for those who are broken, hearts that are eager to obey.

Loving God, we want to be single-minded in our devotion to You. We know that we can do that only with undivided hearts. Give us that kind of heart.

Day 31

DIVINE APPOINTMENTS

*An angel of the Lord spoke to Philip: "Get up and go south
to the road that goes down from Jerusalem to Gaza." (This
is the desert road.) So he got up and went. There was an
Ethiopian man, a eunuch and high official of Candace,
queen of the Ethiopians, who was in charge of her entire
treasury. He had come to worship in Jerusalem and was sitting
in his chariot on his way home, reading the prophet Isaiah
aloud. The Spirit told Philip, "Go and join that chariot."*

ACTS 8:26–29

For a time, we lived in a country where we could not speak the local language. Obviously, that would make sharing Jesus a special challenge. During that time, we came up with a strategy that we thought might work. We would need to take taxis as we traveled around the city—and we agreed Ruth would sit in the back seat of the taxi and pray while Nik would sit in the front seat and hope that God would allow the possibility of a spiritual conversation with the driver. Normally, a passenger would not sit in the front seat, but we were hoping that our unusual seating arrangement would open doors to conversation.

Of course, this strategy was predicated on the driver being able to speak English—so that became a part of our praying as well! It would have been unusual to find an English-speaking driver in this Muslim country, so we were once again asking God to provide something that would have been quite uncommon.

On our first morning in the country, we found a taxi to take us to the marketplace. Amazingly, the taxi driver was able to speak English. As we settled in for our ride to the market, the driver warmly welcomed us to his country.

Then, he turned and asked us a question that we will never forget. In complete seriousness, he said, "I have been waiting for you. I must know . . . what is the meaning of life? Can you tell me what that is?"

I turned and looked at my wife, as if jokingly to say, "You might want to slow down your prayers just a little!"

We had prayed for this kind of opportunity, but still we were stunned. Knowing that this could be a long conversation, I first suggested that the driver slow down. And he did. What should have been a five- or ten-minute ride to the market turned into a forty-minute trip. Unfortunately, the driver kept his taxi meter running the entire time! But we were happy to pay a larger fare for the opportunity to share with this man. For forty minutes, while Ruth prayed, I was able to discuss with this man about "the meaning of life."

We sometimes imagine that witness depends on some creative activity that we initiate or some program that we enact. And those can often be truly helpful in our efforts to share Jesus. All the same, it seems to us that witness is often more about listening and about sensing what God might already be doing in someone's life. We have learned that God is already at work in every place—and already at work in every life—before we ever show up. And it is our responsibility to pay attention, to sense what God is already doing, and to join Him in His work.

Clearly, God had already been working in the life of this taxi driver. Even his question about the meaning of life was God-directed.

And God just happened to put us in the right place on this particular day—in this particular taxi—for this holy conversation.

Sharing Jesus is not only a responsibility; it is also the greatest joy we can have. As we share in God's transforming work, we, at the same time, celebrate the transformation that He has brought to us.

Lord God, we praise You for Your creative ability to do exactly what is needed in the right places at the right times in the right lives! Indeed, You can do anything You desire. You can do anything You choose to do. We call these encounters "divine appointments"—because that is exactly what they are.

We marvel at how You can arrange for Your children to be in a certain taxi in a certain city in a certain country on a certain day speaking with a certain man. Give us eyes to see these divine appointments when You provide them. Then, give us the courage to act and speak boldly as we join You in Your work.

Day 32

NO BARRIERS

When they heard this, they were pierced to the heart and said to Peter and the rest of the apostles: "Brothers, what should we do?"

ACTS 2:37

Our repeated struggles with malaria in Malawi led to our transfer to South Africa. There, we found ourselves in the unusual situation of living as white people in the middle of the black homeland of Transkei in a village called Lady Frere. While many people questioned our decision to live in that area, we knew that it was exactly where God wanted us to be.

Immediately upon our arrival in South Africa, we began to learn the local language of Xhosa. This, too, was unusual. We were told that it was rare for white people to learn the language of a local black population. But we knew that language would be necessary if we wanted to be effective in sharing Jesus.

After about a year of (sometimes hilarious and sometimes painful) struggling with Xhosa, we graduated from our language school. Our teacher had been the very patient Mama Nkuhlu. Several days later, a deacon from a local church, Mr. Mpiti, took us into one of the black townships so that we could share our faith in our newly learned Xhosa. We, of course, were not really ready to do that. Even though we had passed our test, we knew that actually going out and speaking the language was far beyond our ability. Still, we went.

We went to the door of a small house and began talking with a young woman. She was quite surprised to see white faces in her neighborhood, but she was willing to talk with us. She seemed both interested and amused at our efforts to speak Xhosa. As we began to talk with her, Mr. Mpiti slipped away and began another conversation down the street. We were completely on our own!

With our brand-new, unpolished, and untried language skills, we asked the young woman if we could talk to her about Jesus. She told us that she would like to hear about Jesus. For the next twenty minutes, we bumbled and stumbled our way through the story of Jesus. When we asked her if she wanted to follow Jesus, she immediately said, "Yes!"

Because her response came so quickly and so easily, we assumed that she could not have truly understood what we had shared. So we began again and, for another twenty minutes, laboriously shared the story of Jesus. We asked again if she wanted to follow Jesus. Her answer again was the same: "Yes!"

We were still quite sure that she had not understood what we were saying—so we recited the story of Jesus a third time. Once again, she indicated her sincere desire to follow Jesus.

By that time, Mr. Mpiti had returned. In Xhosa, he asked the woman, "Well, how are these white people doing?" She replied, "Well, they are doing fine. But for some reason, they will not let me come to Jesus! I have told them three times that I want to follow Jesus, but they will not let me!" Mr. Mpiti laughed—and, later, never missed the opportunity to tell the story of the new workers and their first experience trying to use the local language.

We love this story—partly because we can laugh at ourselves. More than that, though, the story is a reminder that God has often prepared the heart of a person before we ever show up.

This woman's response to the gospel had very little to do with our language skill—but everything to do with God's previous activity in her life. She was clearly ready to receive Christ; we just happened to be the people who were privileged enough to show up and share the invitation.

Almighty God, thank You for reminding us that You can break down any and every barrier that might separate and divide You from Your people. Thank You for reminding us that You can use our efforts to communicate—even if those efforts are not perfect. Despite the limitations that we might feel, set us free to tell the story of Your goodness and grace.

Lord, we do not always have the opportunity to be part of a person's decision to follow Jesus, but help us never to miss the opportunity to present Your invitation. Even when we cannot see it clearly, we know that it is quite possible that You have prepared this person for the invitation You offer through us.

Day 33

HOW TO MEASURE A LIFE

*For I am already being poured out as a drink offering, and
the time for my departure is close. I have fought the good
fight, I have finished the race, I have kept the faith. There is
reserved for me the crown of righteousness, which the Lord,
the righteous Judge, will give me on that day, and not only
to me, but to all those who have loved his appearing.*

2 TIMOTHY 4:6–8

Several times in this devotional book we have admitted the
sense of failure that we have often carried through our lives.
Looking back, we feel that we worked so very hard and tried our very
best to share Jesus in a broken and lost world. And certainly, we can
point to many parts of our story that we can celebrate and be grateful
for. Still, we know without doubt that we could have done more, and
we could have done better. Surely, we could have been more faithful,
more committed, and more productive.

At this point in our lives, we look back and wonder how to measure our lives. And how God measures our lives. It is good for all of us
to consider what it means to live a faithful and God-honoring life. And
it is also good to be reminded (over and over again!) that God doesn't
measure our lives by how successful we were or how productive we have
been. So-called "success" and measurable "productivity" are blessings
that God might or might not allow us to experience. Even if we cannot

easily identify those things, however, God is most concerned about our hearts and about how fully those hearts have belonged to Him.

Near the end of his life, the apostle Paul reflected on these very things in a letter to young Timothy. Paul was thrilled with the life that he had lived, and he knew that he had been deeply committed to fulfilling God's call on his life. Still, he wished that he could have done more!

Reflecting on his life, however, Paul said that he had fought well, that he had run a good race, that he had been true to the faith. He knew that the ultimate assessment of his life—the only assessment of his life that would matter—would come from God. Paul was willing to place his effort and his obedience in God's hands—and trust what God would say about how Paul had lived his life.

It was not, of course, a matter of earning God's favor or doing something to impress God. No, Paul knew that every part of his story was a matter of God's grace. Yet, responding to God's grace, Paul knew the joy of strenuous effort, the joy of striving, the joy of doing his best.

Most of us probably have much time still to serve God. Most of us likely have many more opportunities ahead in the race that is still to come. We can decide in these next days to serve deeply, to sacrifice well, and to love Jesus with all that we are, and all that we have.

All of that, of course, is a response to His grace. But all of that also demonstrates the depth of our love for Him.

Lord God, we know that we cannot earn Your favor. We know that we cannot live in a way that would cause You to love us more. By Your grace, You have already determined to love us with an everlasting love. So we know that what You have done—and not what we do—is what matters.

Even so, we choose to live our lives in response to Your great love. We are so grateful to You that we cannot help but respond to Your grace. As we do that, help us to run a good race. Help us to fight a good fight. Help us to keep the faith. Help us to care most about the things that matter most to You.

We are tempted to measure our lives. But we confess that we often use the wrong standards. Set us free from the burdens of what we consider success and productivity— and simply trust You to do all that You want to do with hearts that belong more and more completely to You.

Day 34

Single-Minded

Sanballat and Geshem sent me [Nehemiah] a message: "Come, let's meet together in the villages of the Ono Valley." They were planning to harm me. So I sent messengers to them, saying, "I am doing important work and cannot come down. Why should the work cease while I leave it and go down to you?" Four times they sent me the same proposal, and I gave them the same reply.

Nehemiah 6:2–4

Persecuted by government officials with the support and cooperation of the established church in his country, a follower of Jesus named Constantine[3] was put in prison and subjected to intense physical and psychological torture. Persecutors wanted very much to see believers renounce their faith. Even if that did not happen, the persecutors tried to destroy the soul and the self-identity of their prisoners.

When he shared his story with us, Constantine talked about his abuse in prison in a straightforward, matter-of-fact way. Even though he was describing experiences that had happened a long time ago, the pain in his voice was raw. He was especially disappointed that the traditional church in his country had been party to his imprisonment. His grief was even deeper when he learned in prison that his wife had died. Looking back, he wondered how he had even found the strength to carry on.

"I wrote many songs," Constantine said. "God gave me words and melodies to strengthen and soothe my soul. The whole time I was in prison, I was writing songs."

"How many songs did you write?" we asked.

He smiled and replied, "About six hundred."

Many years later, the name of Constantine is still well known throughout his country. Even today, believers in this country continue to sing Constantine's songs when they gather for worship. Somehow, despite intense suffering, Constantine's music had kept him alive—and Constantine's music continues to strengthen the church.

In the face of such cruel torture and abuse, it would have been easy for Constantine to lose focus. It would have been easy for Constantine to grow cold and careless with his faith. It would have been easy for Constantine to give in to despair and discouragement.

But just like Nehemiah in the Old Testament, Constantine maintained his focus on the work that God had given him—the work that God had given to him even in prison. He refused to be pulled away from that work. Even the abuse of his persecutors did not distract Constantine from his calling to faithfulness.

Nehemiah's work was to build the wall—and he was relentlessly committed to its completion. Even when others attempted to pull him away from his task, Nehemiah remained true to his call. "I am doing a great work!" he said. Despite repeated attempts to distract him from his calling, Nehemiah refused to allow anything to keep him from the work that God had given.

In a similar way, God had given Constantine work to do. In essence, Constantine's work was simply to stay true to God—and through his music and devotion and worship, that is exactly what Constantine did. For generations, Constantine's single-minded faithfulness has produced fruit in the life of the church.

God, we tend to live our lives all over the place. If people were to ask us what our purpose was, we're not sure what exactly we would say. Often, we have no idea what our purpose is. Most days, we simply want to survive. So we hear the stories of Nehemiah and Constantine with a measure of envy. We sincerely wish we could be sure about our purpose. We wish that we could have a purpose so grand that it would consume us.

We suspect that You smile when you hear us say those words, because You have given us a purpose that is plenty grand. You have given us a purpose that is worth our very lives. You tell us that our purpose is to walk with You, to love You completely, to tell Your story, and to share Your grace. Help us to give ourselves so fully to that purpose that we might be single-minded, passionate, consumed.

Show us the purpose for which we were created. Then empower us to embrace that purpose fully.

Day 35

EYES THAT CAN SEE

*When the servant of the man of God got up early and went out,
he discovered an army with horses and chariots surrounding
the city. So he asked Elisha, "Oh, my master, what are we to
do?" Elisha said, "Don't be afraid, for those who are with us
outnumber those who are with them." Then Elisha prayed,
"LORD, please open his eyes and let him see." So the LORD
opened the servant's eyes, and he saw that the mountain was
covered with horses and chariots of fire all around Elisha.*

2 KINGS 6:15–17

✝ God has a way of equipping and empowering His people
regardless of the persecution and suffering that they might
face. During the 1950s, persecution directed toward followers of Jesus
in the Soviet Union was severe. Believers generally could not gather
openly or in large groups; instead, they met in small communities that
we normally call house churches.

These small groups were certainly "churches"—they fulfilled
every function that would be part of any church. At the same time,
though, these gathered groups were typically very small. Often, in fact,
a house church might be comprised of an extended family: a father,
a mother, a few children, and maybe an uncle and an aunt. In that
world, "church" would seem awfully small—and, because of security
concerns, it would be difficult to catch even a glimpse of what God
might be doing with other people or what God might be doing in

other places. An unexpected principle about persecution is, if we do our security so efficient that the persecutors cannot find us, other believers will not know of us also!

Even today, we might assume that same perspective. We might focus so much on what God is doing in our little corner of the world that we forget that He is also at work in other places, with other people. Our spiritual vision can be terribly small and limited.

To address that limited point of view, several Russian pastors in the 1950s thought that it would be a good idea to gather young people from different house churches to help them get a sense of God's activity, which was so much grander and larger than what they were experiencing in their isolated small groups. Even though it was dangerous (and even though many people considered it foolish), these pastors organized a youth congress in Moscow with this purpose in mind. They knew that the authorities would notice, but they still thought it was worth the risk.

(And sure enough, the authorities *did* notice! When the gathering was finished, the three pastors were arrested and sentenced to prison for three years.)

Before that happened, though, seven hundred young followers of Jesus from several hundred house churches gathered in Moscow for a few days. It turned out to be a remarkable and powerful gathering. Many good things happened during that short time, but what might have been most important was catching a glimpse of the immense activity of God beyond what each small house church could see on its own. Together, these young believers saw that God was doing so much more than they ever imagined.

As we think about this gathering in the Soviet Union, we are reminded of the story of Elisha's servant, told in 2 Kings 6. This servant's spiritual vision was limited. He was unable to see or sense the activity of God. When Elisha prayed that God would open the eyes of his servant, the servant saw things that he had not seen before. God was present; God was at work; God had things well in hand.

Despite what we see with our eyes—and despite our limited point of view—there is a deeper reality that we often fail to see. While interviewing believers around the world—repeatedly—persecuted followers of Jesus seemed to talk with Jesus *as if He were really present.* They seemed to see things that other people couldn't see. They seemed to sense God's activity as something completely real and certain. In a word, they seemed to have spiritual eyes . . . that could see.

And we would be wise to open our eyes—and our hearts—to that deeper reality.

Often, it seems, we have vision problems. We cannot see what is right before our eyes.

These young believers in Russia were offered a glimpse of what God was doing in other places—and they went home renewed, encouraged, and filled with hope. Because of what they had seen, everything was changed.

Lord God, we simply don't see it. We look around and we see only trouble. We look around and we see only limitation. We see impossibility. We see defeat. We have such trouble seeing You and anything that You are doing. Like the servant in the Bible story, we confess that we have poor spiritual vision.

*Open our eyes. Show us what is true. Help us to see You and what
You are doing. We long to believe that You are present and at
work. We long to take the promises of Scripture to heart. We long
to believe everything that Jesus says. We long to be convinced that
this entire world is brimming with Your vital presence and power.*

We are so tired of our limited sight. Open our eyes.

Day 36

COMMANDED

*Even when the cloud stayed over the tabernacle many
days, the Israelites carried out the LORD's requirement and
did not set out. Sometimes the cloud remained over the
tabernacle for only a few days. They would camp at the
LORD's command and set out at the LORD's command.*

NUMBERS 9:19–20

Looking back, our mission pilgrimage seems to have been often shaped by circumstances. In every case, however, we knew that even those circumstances were orchestrated by God Himself.

We sensed God's clear call to serve in Malawi—and we sensed a confirmation of that call throughout our time there. While we would have happily remained in Malawi for decades, struggles with malaria forced us to find a new place of service.

From Malawi, we went to the Transkei, one of the black homelands in South Africa during apartheid. During our time there, we experienced a wonderful ministry and received a life-changing education in matters of race. It was during this season that we re-read carefully and prayerfully the book of Acts. God used that time of prayerful searching to place on our hearts the need to serve in a place where people had not yet encountered the gospel.

Responding to the clear call of God, we moved to Kenya, where we could access unreached and unengaged people groups throughout the Horn of Africa. Once again, we were certain that God had put us exactly where He wanted us to be.

Later, during our time of visiting and interviewing persecuted believers around the globe, we sensed the hand of God even in our travel preparations. We felt that God was arranging the details as He led us to people who could host our visits, provide translation, and open doors for contacts with believers in persecution (many of whom were in hiding). In many cases, these encounters seemed providential, mysterious, and even miraculous.

Somehow—and without fail—God leads His people. We might struggle to know when it is time to act and when it is time to wait—when it is time to go and when it is time to stay—but God assures us that He will provide guidance and direction. God obviously wants His people to obey. And He assures us that He will help us understand exactly what obedience will look like.

In Numbers 9, God's people are given clear instructions about the guidance of God. Sometimes the people are expected to stay right where they are and simply wait. Sometimes the people are expected to get up and go. Sometimes the time of waiting is long and extended; sometimes the time of waiting is relatively short. Day by day, the circumstances are different—and God's people cannot presume to know what God might ask of them.

But one thing is certain: God will lead His people. The repeated phrase in Numbers 9 is "at the LORD's command." God does not expect us to guess about the right course of action—or merely hope that we are getting it right. Rather, God tells us what to do. "At the LORD's command," we sometimes stay put. And "at the LORD's command," we sometimes set out.

Whatever it is that we do, we want it to be "at the LORD's command."

The Israelites in Numbers 9 relied on the visual image of a cloud that represented the presence of God. Today, we generally don't have a cloud to give us direction, but God still finds ways to make His guidance clear.

In response, we might go to Malawi or to the Transkei or to the Horn of Africa or to a multitude of countries around the world.

Or we might go across the street or across town or across the ocean. Whatever we do, we do it "at the LORD's command."

Lord God, we hunger to hear Your voice. Even as we listen for a new word, help us to faithfully obey what You have already said to us. When You tell us to be still, we will be still. When You tell us to speak, we will speak. When You tell us to stay put, we will stay put. And when You tell us to go, we will go.

Give us a heart that is eager to obey. Help us to pay careful attention to the many ways that You speak. Then, give us the courage to act, respond, and obey.

Day 37

SORROW-BEARING

"Blessed are those who mourn, for they will be comforted."
MATTHEW 5:4

✝ One of our greatest struggles was deciding what to do in response to the suffering that seemed to be all around us. Whether we were in Malawi, Transkei, or the Horn of Africa—and even when we were in Europe or the United States–it seemed that profound suffering was always present. Today it is still present all over the world.

The causes of suffering are many: war, poverty, natural disaster, broken relationships, economic breakdown, loneliness, and drought quickly come to mind. Often, suffering is the result of evil and destructive behavior.

It was not especially difficult to see the suffering—or even to name the sources and causes—what was far more difficult for us was deciding exactly what to do in response. We knew that we could not simply ignore the needs that we saw. But we also knew that wise and strategic choices would be required. Even more, we knew that our response would grow out of our desire to act like Jesus.

In Matthew 5:4, Jesus talks about the blessedness of mourning. Obviously, we mourn when we lose a loved one—and that is one part of what Jesus is describing here. Mourning is also something that we do (and something we *should* do) when we become aware of our sin—which is another part of what Jesus mentions. But probably at the heart of Jesus' words here is the mourning we do on behalf of other people.

Jesus is describing the condition of people with kingdom hearts. Among so many other characteristics, Jesus tells us that people who are part of His kingdom mourn on behalf of other people. Even more specifically, we mourn most for those who are not yet part of God's kingdom. We mourn for broken and shattered lives. We grieve when we see hurt and pain and abuse and injustice. We grieve when we see children who don't have a chance. And we certainly grieve when we grasp the fact that many people in our world have never had the opportunity to hear about Jesus.

On the one hand, that is simply the way the world is. On the other hand, that reality should never fail to break our hearts.

When Martin Luther was translating the Greek New Testament into German, he struggled with this second Beatitude. He was not exactly sure how to translate the words. He wondered: what German word should he use to translate "mourn"? He settled on the German word *Leidtragen*–a word that literally means "sorrow-bearing." "Blessed are the sorrow-bearers!" Luther wrote.

> *Blessed are those who bear their own sorrow—and blessed are those who bear the sorrows of others.*

How wonderful that we, the people of God, should be known as sorrow-bearers. And how wonderful that our sorrow-bearing is intended to be done in community. The apostle Paul tells us to mourn with those who mourn (Rom. 12:15). We are plainly instructed in Galatians 6:2 to carry each other's burdens. What causes one person pain is a deep concern to the entire community, and the entire family of God is privileged to help carry that burden. Our mourning, our sorrow-bearing, is best done in community.

Ruth often says that there is no such thing as a free church and a persecuted church. There is simply the church—one church—at all times free and at all times persecuted.

Even more, we are told that God Himself joins in our mourning. Describing the coming Messiah, Isaiah used this language: "He himself bore our sicknesses, and he carried our pains" (Isa. 53:4).

During his season of waiting for the Christ, Simeon was "looking forward to Israel's consolation" (Luke 2:25). Simeon was waiting for the One who would bring comfort. Jesus is the One who has come to *console* His people. So when we grieve and mourn—when we carry in our hearts the suffering of the world—we do that with one another— and we do that with our Lord Himself.

What do we do with all the suffering that surrounds us?

We carry it. We carry it together. And we carry it with God.

Indeed: *"Blessed are those who mourn, for they will be comforted."*

God of all comfort, we place the suffering of this entire world into Your gracious and able hands.

We grieve for our own sin. We grieve for the sin of others. And we grieve especially for the brokenness and heartache of this world. We mourn with those who mourn. We mourn for those who do not yet know You.

We ask you to carry the suffering that is too heavy for us—but we also ask that You would help us to be sorrow-bearers.

Give us the courage not to look away. Give us the courage to feel deeply. Give us the courage to pray for those who suffer.

Day 38

MOVING THE STONES

Then Jesus, deeply moved again, came to the tomb. It was a
cave, and a stone was lying against it. "Remove the stone,"
Jesus said. Martha, the dead man's sister, told him, "Lord,
there is already a stench because he has been dead four days."
Jesus said to her, "Didn't I tell you that if you believed you
would see the glory of God?" So they removed the stone.

JOHN 11:38–41A

The spread of the gospel is sometimes described in Scripture using the imagery of planting. Someone sows the seed; another person waters. Then, after the plant grows, there is harvesting. That's a great picture of the spiritual growth that can happen in the life of an individual.

In Somalia, we rarely felt that we were involved in that specific process. Instead, another image comes to mind: We were simply moving stones so that a seed could possibly be planted there some day in the future.

That image is especially fitting for Somalia. Not only is much of Somali a desert region—it is also a desert region that is covered with rocks. The topography is unforgiving, desolate, and harsh. Before any planting can take place, the ground must first be prepared. The first step is to remove the massive number of stones that litter the landscape.

This first step is often exactly how we saw our work in Somalia. We were moving stones in the hope that one day something might be planted there. While we understand that moving the stones was essential and necessary, we discovered that the work of moving stones was tedious, difficult, and painful.

That same image shows up in John 11. The Bible story begins with devastating loss; Lazarus has died. If we are familiar with the story, we know that Jesus is about to do something in response to that painful loss—He is about to raise Lazarus from the dead.

Before He does that, however, Jesus says, "Remove the stone" (John 11:38). That simple detail—that simple word of instruction—that simple command—is extremely important. Jesus knew that there were things that He alone could do. But He also knew that there were things that others could do. In this instruction, Jesus is inviting others to join in the work.

And, evidently, one thing we can do . . . is remove stones.

As the story unfolds, we see that Mary has some valid reasons for not removing the stone that guards the tomb of Lazarus. "It's going to smell bad," she essentially says. "This will be ugly. This will get complicated. This will not be neat and tidy. Frankly, Jesus, this promises to be a big mess."

But Jesus simply says: "Remove the stone."

In other words, "You do what you can do—and I will do what I alone can do!"

This is a beautiful picture that defines so much of our story. We did not often get to do the planting and the watering and the harvesting. But we sure got to move plenty of stones. And though we never saw much fruit, we knew that planting would never be possible unless the stones were moved.

Miracle-working God, give us the courage to join in. Give us the courage to do what we can do. Forgive us for being so sure about how exactly things will turn out. Forgive us for being so sure about the end of the story. Help us to see possibility and hope in Your invitation to do what we can do.

We know that You could have chosen to do everything without our help. But what grace there is in You choosing us to partner with You anyway! Like children "helping" a parent, we will joyfully overcome our excuses and will do just what You command. Thank You for allowing us to move stones. Thank You for allowing us to share in activities that open doors for Your miracles.

Day 39

LIVING MOMENT BY MOMENT

For me, to live is Christ and to die is gain.

PHILIPPIANS 1:21

✝ Several years ago, we heard a gripping testimony from inside a country in the Middle East. A young overseas worker was sharing about a recent tragedy in her family. In a horrific accident, she and her husband had suddenly lost their two young children and her husband's mother. The young woman's grief was overwhelming.

Several months after the accident, she stood before her spiritual family and shared her heart. With halting words and painful bursts of emotion, she spoke of God's faithfulness and she spoke of her own broken heart.

And the honesty of her testimony is something we will never forget.

This was not a sugarcoated testimony. The young woman had no easy answers. Clearly, she was clinging to her God. At the same time, though, she questioned what had happened and she questioned what she would do next. Her intention was to return to her place of service. Her intention was to continue serving God. But she openly confessed how very hard that would be. And she honestly wondered if she would be able to do it.

Every person who heard her speak was deeply moved. It probably wasn't the most eloquent testimony we have ever heard, but it certainly was one of the most powerful.

As she concluded her testimony, this grieving mother quoted the words of Philippians 1:21: *"For me, to live is Christ and to die is gain."* That verse reflects the apostle Paul's ambivalence about what would be best for the cause of Christ in his own life. Paul knew that if he died, he would immediately be with his Lord. That would be a good thing. But Paul also knew that if he continued to live, he could be useful in service to his Lord. And that too would be a good thing. Paul was content to leave the outcome in God's hands.

Dying for Christ is *not* where this grieving mother found her struggle. She was already willing to die for Christ—she said that she had settled that a long time before. But given the unspeakable loss that she had recently experienced, she didn't know if she would be able to live for Christ! Through her tears, she wondered how she would be able to carry on without her two precious children.

It was a sobering and honest word.

It's quite possible for us to be willing to die for our Lord. And one day in the future, we might have to face that possibility. In the meantime, however, we have the challenge to live for our Lord.

It is one thing to face a possibility that might never happen; it is another thing altogether to make a choice that we face . . . today.

Sacrifices are not always grand and glorious. Sacrifices are not always the stuff of movies and books. Sometimes, the sacrifices that are necessary and required are the little, moment-by-moment choices and decisions that we make every day.

Those choices and decisions reveal who we are. More than that, those choices and decisions reveal Who it is that we are living for.

Should it ever happen, Lord, we pray that we will be willing to lay down our lives for You. In the meantime, however, we declare that we are willing to live for You.

Today. Now. Here. In this moment.

Forgive us for imagining that we would be willing to make some grand sacrifice for You—even while we hesitate to give up so little right now. Teach us to value You more than anything else. Teach us to value obedience to Your call more than anything else.

Day 40

THE CERTAINTY OF PERSECUTION

Dear friends, don't be surprised when the fiery ordeal comes
among you to test you as if something unusual were happening
to you. Instead, rejoice as you share in the sufferings of Christ,
so that you may also rejoice with great joy when his glory is
revealed. . . . So then, let those who suffer according to God's will
entrust themselves to a faithful Creator while doing what is good.

1 PETER 4:12–13, 19

Until we spent time with persecuted followers of Jesus around the world, our understanding of persecution was simple and unquestioned: We believed that persecution could be avoided and that persecution was completely unnecessary.

Many Christians who were raised and reared in the American church have conveniently ignored both the clear teaching of Scripture regarding persecution and the straight talk of Jesus Himself. It took a group of Russian pastors to help us see the truth.

Listening to them share their stories, we were forced to see persecution in an entirely different way. They used the phrases almost casually:

"I was in prison for seven years."

"I remember being beaten and forced to sleep naked in a cold, damp cell."

"I'll never forget how the church cared for my family while I was in prison."

As they told their stories, we felt as if we were hearing the stories of Scripture come to life. Captivated, we demanded to know why their stories had not been written down, recorded, documented, and shared.

"The world needs to hear about your faith," we pleaded. "Why haven't you collected your stories and put them in a book? Your stories rival movies made by Hollywood."

An older pastor rose and stood in front of the large window in the front room of the house. He asked quietly, "How many times have you gathered your children, taken them to a window in your home that faces east, and told them to get ready because the sun was about to come up in the east?"

It seemed like a silly question. My reply, "The sun always comes up in the east—so there would be nothing unusual about that. And there would be no reason to point out the rising of the sun to our children!"

"That is why," the older pastor explained, "we have not put our stories in books. Because there is nothing unusual about our persecution. It is just like the sun coming up in the east. It happens all the time—and it is exactly what we would expect. Persecution for our faith has always been—and it probably always will be—a normal part of life."

Written against the backdrop of persecution, 1 Peter tells us the same thing: *Followers of Jesus will face persecution.*

Earlier, Jesus had promised His followers that they would not be loved by the world. He had trained His followers how to react and respond to the attacks from the world. Even more than that, Jesus had suggested that there is a kind of "blessedness" that accompanies persecution (Matt. 5:10–12). In this same chapter Jesus tells His disciples that they would be arrested and that He was sending them to the authorities in order to be a witness! And the words of 1 Peter are right in line with Jesus' teaching. This part of Scripture deals with all kinds of suffering—but it focuses most clearly on the suffering that happens because of a relationship with Jesus.

Peter is writing to believers who are finding life to be unbelievably hard. So he says to them, "Do not be surprised! Do not be surprised by the painful trials that you are suffering. Do not be surprised by your fiery ordeal. Do not be surprised by the attacks. Do not be surprised *as if* this is something strange or unexpected or unusual. This is simply part of following Jesus. It comes with the territory—and you have no reason to believe that you will be exempt."

In other words, persecution for followers of Jesus is . . . just like the sun coming up in the east.

We generally want to believe that all suffering—and especially the suffering related to persecution—is *contrary* to God's will. But these verses in Matthew 10 and 1 Peter make it clear that there is a suffering that is *according to God's will*. That kind of suffering is fully within the will of God and it is a kind of suffering that can be used by God for His purposes.

God, it is, frankly, difficult to imagine that suffering for Jesus is a privilege. We are not ready to accept this. We prefer, instead, to see suffering as something to be avoided. Yet the words of Scripture—and the stories of believers in persecution—haunt us. We are clearly invited—and we are clearly expected—to share in Jesus' sufferings.

We figure that, if we stay really quiet, we might be able to avoid persecution. But we cannot stay quiet about our love for Jesus. So we find ourselves in a tough place: we want to avoid the suffering that Jesus said was sure to come to all who follow Him—but we know that we can avoid suffering only by being quiet about Jesus.

Help us to understand that suffering for You is a privilege. Help us to understand that suffering for You is an opportunity to bring You glory. We surely do not seek suffering, Lord. But we choose to be open about our love for You no matter what the cost.

Give us courage.

Day 41

LOVING OUR PERSECUTORS

*"You have heard that it was said, Love your neighbor
and hate your enemy. But I tell you, love your enemies
and pray for those who persecute you, so that you
may be children of your Father in heaven."*

MATTHEW 5:43–45A

Often the best learning happened in our teaching when we
had completed our formal presentations and simply invited
questions and conversation. That certainly happened one night in
Sudan. The question itself broke our hearts; one of the women asked,
"When they beat us for our faith, can we fight back?"

We allowed the question to hang in the air as the gathered group
struggled about how to answer.

The men in the group spoke first. "Of course, you must fight
back!" they said. "If you do not fight back, it will get worse and worse.
No one will blame you for fighting back!"

That seemed like an obvious answer, until several of the women
offered a different view: "But we must remember what Jesus taught
us. We must love those who hurt us. We must not fight back!" These
women called to mind what Jesus did on the cross when He offered
forgiveness to His tormentors.

A thoughtful, tender conversation ensued. We were able to share
stories of how other believers, though persecuted in other parts of the
world, had addressed this very real problem. What seemed to startle the

group the most was the suggestion that the best way to end persecution was to ask God to transform the persecutors into brothers and sisters in Christ. By helping persecutors find Jesus, persecution would come to an end. And that would happen not by running away from the persecutors or fighting the persecutors—but by loving the persecutors, praying for them, and sharing Jesus with them.

Persecuted followers of Jesus in China, in particular, saw this approach as intensely practical. Even more, they saw this approach as a mark of spiritual maturity. These believers in China prayed that God would give them a supernatural ability to love those who were causing them such pain. They asked God to change the way they saw their persecutors.

These believers in Sudan were captivated by this new thought. In fact, they said that they had never thought about this approach—and they said that no one had ever suggested that they treat their persecutors this way.

Four biological brothers *immediately* began to leave our gathering. We were not finished for the evening, but they stood up and prepared to leave.

When we asked them where they were going, they said matter-of-factly, "We are going right now to share Jesus with our families who persecute us. After we win them to Jesus, we will come back and learn some more."

Lord God, it is simply in our nature to fight back. It is simply in our nature to pay back those who cause us pain. We have been trained by the world to respond to others in the same way

that they treat us. So Your expectation that we love and pray for the people who do us harm is hard for us to hear. The very thought of sharing Jesus with a persecutor makes no sense to us.

At the same time, we know full well that You want to set us free from what comes naturally. You want to empower us to love freely, widely, broadly. You want us to treat others not the way they have treated us—but to treat them the way that You have treated us! Set us free from our stubborn tendency to decide for ourselves who exactly deserves Your grace and who doesn't. Remind us that we do not deserve Your grace either.

Help us to respond immediately when You teach us something again and again and again.

Day 42

Free to Say Yes

Then I heard the voice of the Lord asking: "Who should I send? Who will go for us?" I said: "Here I am. Send me."
Isaiah 6:8

Our call to serve overseas was overwhelming in its simplicity and its clarity. As a young married couple, we were open to serve God anywhere in the world. In His grace, God confirmed that call and provided a clear path as we tried our best to be faithful to Him.

At one point, early in the 1980s, we hosted an overseas speaker at our church in Kentucky. Even though we were seated in different parts of the sanctuary—and even though we didn't talk with one another beforehand—we both responded by coming forward that evening to renew our commitment to serve overseas. We had each felt God speaking to us about the same thing at the very same time. That evening, we made a decision to begin the overseas appointment application process immediately.

The application process proved to be challenging and time-consuming, but our sense of command and call were strong and certain. When we read the words of the Great Commission, we understood immediately that Jesus intended those words for every one of His followers—and we knew immediately that those words were intended for us. Some people might describe that interpretation of Scripture as naïve—but we were absolutely convinced that it was our responsibility to share in the assignment of the Great Commission: to go and to make disciples. We were completely convinced that, as followers of Jesus, that was our life assignment.

We did everything that we could do—and we fulfilled every expectation that was placed before us—so that we could go and make disciples.

We left for Malawi on New Year's Day, 1984. It seemed that we were living out a Bible story: saying good-bye to family and friends, leaving everything that we knew, going to a place we had never seen before, trusting God to provide for us and lead the way. Looking back, we are sure that we were anxious and concerned, but the feelings we remember most about those days are joy and contentment—and a deep and abiding sense that we were doing exactly what God had commanded us to do. What adventure was unfolding before us!

The Bible is filled with stories of God's call. Within each of those call stories is the response of the person being called. Some people, such as Isaiah and Ezekiel, respond with willing submission—even enthusiasm: "Here I am, Lord! I am ready and willing!"

Others, such as Gideon and Jeremiah—and especially Moses— have some concerns. In fact, they respond to God's call by highlighting all the reasons that His call is not a good idea. Even though they eventually obey, their first response is a reluctance.

In our case, we were simply thrilled to know that God wanted to use us.

And we celebrated the fact that we were free to say, "Yes!"

Frankly, God, we can think of many reasons why we should not embrace Your call. We sense that it may be too costly for us to obey You. But we also realize how costly it will be for us to disobey. Even so, answering Your call will mean that we will need to sacrifice. It might mean that we will need to go. Or it might mean that we will need to stay where we already are.

Whatever happens, it will mean that we will need to change—and we would rather things stay the same.

And yet . . . we hear Your voice. And our excuses suddenly feel so empty and so vacant. Despite our fears and hesitation, we want so much to say yes. And we praise You for the freedom that allows us to do just that.

We are Your servants. Teach us that life is defined by Your command and by our response to Your call.

Day 43

LIGHT AND MOMENTARY TROUBLES

*Therefore we do not give up. Even though our outer person
is being destroyed, our inner person is being renewed day
by day. For our momentary light affliction is producing for
us an absolutely incomparable eternal weight of glory. So
we do not focus on what is seen, but on what is unseen. For
what is seen is temporary, but what is unseen is eternal.*

2 CORINTHIANS 4:16–18

Pastor Chang was eighty-three years old when we encountered him. He had been in and out of prison multiple times, and had been released from his latest incarceration just a few days before we met him. Pastor Chang had spent his entire life preaching and teaching the gospel, and he had paid a high cost for that privilege.

He first went to prison for three years when he became a follower of Jesus. After being released from that first imprisonment, Pastor Chang went to prison again (for three more years) for sharing Jesus with other people and for starting a church. He was sent to prison once again for another three years for being a leader in a house-church movement. Each time Pastor Chang was released from prison, he simply returned to his ministry and continued preaching, teaching, and sharing his faith.

Pastor Chang reminded us of the apostle Paul. Just as Paul had invested his life in young Timothy, Pastor Chang had invested his life in young evangelists and church planters who could carry on his work and ministry. Even though his own ministry was productive and effective, he knew that his ministry would be even greater if he could mentor other followers of Jesus to embrace the work that he was doing.

It was a holy privilege to listen to Pastor Chang talk about his life. It was even more moving to hear stories from the men that Pastor Chang had mentored. These men were his "Timothys." He had led them to faith in Jesus. He had taught them how to evangelize and plant house churches. And, then, he had watched as they grew in faith and obedience. These men had even followed Pastor Chang's example of being arrested and imprisoned for sharing their faith!

We met Pastor Chang three days after his release from prison due to issues with high blood pressure. The Communists did not want him to die a martyr in their prison system, so they released him because of his poor health.

Despite decades of intense suffering, Pastor Chang celebrated what God had done in his life. He owned nothing but the clothes on his back and one extra pair of underwear. He had no home, no retirement account, no car, and no surviving family to care for him. He simply went from house church to house church—possibly anticipating the next time that he would be arrested for his obedience to Jesus. Yet to us, he seemed to be the most joy-filled, richest man on earth.

To believers in the West, Pastor Chang's life of suffering seems unbearable. To Pastor Chang, however, his troubles were light and momentary—nothing at all compared to the glory of walking with Jesus.

That is exactly how the apostle Paul saw his hardships. As significant as his suffering was, Paul refused to dwell on it. Instead, he found a way to focus on what God was doing. Even if it is a challenge for us to describe serious troubles as "light and momentary," we are called to believe that God can use even our troubles for a higher purpose.

Like the apostle Paul, Pastor Chang never denied the pain of his suffering. Instead of focusing on that suffering, though, he found a way to highlight the power and purpose of God. He knew firsthand that God could use light and momentary troubles—as well as heavy and long-lasting troubles—to build His kingdom.

By the time we met Pastor Chang, his blood pressure had returned to normal. Evidently God had plans to use this marvelous man of God a little longer!

God, we want to obey You, but we want You to
meet our needs and fix our troubles first.

But You tell us that You want us to start sharing our faith even while
our challenges continue. God, we want You to do things differently.
We want You to get rid of all those hard things that fill our lives—
and then we will start obeying You. Lord, is it not normal to want
the best for ourselves and those we love? Are we to trade all that we
feel we are entitled to have for the uncertainty of following You?

How can we believe that You are able to use even the
hard things to accomplish what You desire?

Teach us to look at life and especially at our needs and
troubles in a different light. Set us free from our desire
to want everything to be right before we obey.

Day 44

PREOCCUPIED WITH PLACE

*"But you will receive power when the Holy Spirit has come
on you, and you will be my witnesses in Jerusalem, in
all Judea and Samaria, and to the end of the earth."*

ACTS 1:8

It is easy to become preoccupied with geography.

In our case, we can trace our mission pilgrimage this way:
working with churches in Indiana and Kentucky, serving in Malawi,
ministering in the Transkei, living in Kenya while working with the
Somali people, then traveling the world to learn from persecuted followers of Jesus. The flow of our story can easily be reduced to a list of
places.

What all those places have in common, though, is the opportunity
to share Jesus with those who do not know Him yet.

It is possible to imagine that sharing Jesus is limited to a certain
place or a specific geographic location.

For example, we might think: *I'll start to share Jesus when I find
my mission field.* Or we might think: *Sharing Jesus is something that best
happens overseas—but certainly not right here in my neighborhood.*

If we think those things, we are in error.

Jesus' words of commission that we read in Acts 1:8 place the
entire world at our doorstep. Jesus commands us to go to the entire
world! Much to our surprise, Jesus evidently expects His followers to
be His witnesses close by and far away—and everywhere in between.

Our *Jerusalem* is what is most familiar to us. Interestingly, this might be the most difficult place to share our faith—because this is where we are best known. There is no way to share Jesus anonymously in Jerusalem; everybody knows us here!

Judea expands the circle. Judea might still be relatively familiar, but stepping into Judea will expose us to different cultures and backgrounds. Judea might, in fact, be just across the street or down the road, but we will likely encounter different perspectives even in those close places. Judea often contains a different race of people and confronts the racism in all of us.

Samaria will be less familiar. Even though it might be close geographically, going to Samaria will connect us with the lives of people we probably do not know well. Even more, going to Samaria will likely lead us into a world that we might consider "foreign." Going to Samaria will require that we deal with prejudices that we might have. In Samaria, we will be required to confront our own perspectives and nationalism that could potentially inhibit and limit our witness.

And *the end of the earth?* We probably see the end of the earth as so unreachable that going there seems impossible. And when Jesus spoke these words in Acts 1:8, it might have been truly impossible for His followers to reach the end of the earth. But that is not impossible today—unless we are unwilling to obey the clear instruction of Jesus. Jesus fully expects His followers to go to the end of the earth.

Jesus' words remind us that there is no part of the world that is beyond the reach of His grace. And His words remind us that there is no geographic boundary that would limit our sharing. Our response of obedience to His call is not limited to certain places. When we answer Jesus' call by telling Him up front about the places that we would *never* consider going—or the human needs that we could *never* address—or the conditions that would be required for our obedience—we should realize that we have already started down the wrong path.

How much better it is to simply tell Jesus that we are His, that His command is clear, and that our obedience is certain.

Once we do that, we leave matters of geography in His hands.

God, Your vision is broad and expansive. Your plan is comprehensive. Your desire is that all nations bow before You in worship. You invite us to embrace that vision and that plan. But our vision is small. We struggle to wrap our minds and our hearts around Your plan. What You are attempting to accomplish is too grand for our understanding.

We want to argue about places and possibilities; we want to tell You what makes sense and what we are willing to do. All the while, You wait for us simply to surrender. Lord God, help us to trust You. Help us to understand that once we are settled about Your call, we are free to leave every other detail in Your hands.

Doing that feels like freedom. But doing that also scares us.

We are afraid that You might send us to the wrong place. We are afraid that You might not take account of our fears and our desires. We are afraid that You might ignore our list of places that are off-limits.

In those fears, we realize that we do not fully trust You. Forgive us. Remind us that You know what is best. Give us a bigger heart. Give us bigger eyes. Give us more trust.

Day 45

THE MAN ON THE CROSS

*Adopt the same attitude as that of Christ Jesus, who, existing in
the form of God, did not consider equality with God as something
to be exploited. Instead he emptied himself by assuming the
form of a servant, taking on the likeness of humanity. And
when he had come as a man, he humbled himself by becoming
obedient to the point of death—even to death on a cross.*

PHILIPPIANS 2:5–8

One persecuted follower of Jesus in Central Asia agreed to
an interview on the condition that we would never see his
face nor try to learn anything about his background. So we met in a
small room where this man was completely hidden from us. Though
we could not see the man, we could hear him clearly. For six hours, he
told us his story.

For years, this man had been the leader of a group of soldiers
charged with the task of repelling foreign invaders. By his own admission, he took great joy in killing infidels in the name of Allah. He
described these killings in graphic detail.

Eventually, this man began having a dream that repeated itself
over and over again. In the dream, he saw blood on his hands that he
could not wash away. He began to see the blood in his waking hours,
and he recognized this as the blood of all those he had killed. Finally,
one night his dream changed. A man appeared and said, "I am Jesus

the Messiah. I can get the blood off of your hands—if you will just find Me and follow Me."

It took the man a year to find a Bible. It took him even longer to understand what he was reading in that book. He traveled within three countries seeking the Jesus of his dreams. After years of struggling and searching, the man gave his life to Jesus and began to follow Him. He said that, at that point, his repeated dream stopped immediately.

Led by the Holy Spirit and led by his personal study of the Bible, this man learned how to follow Jesus. As he explained it, he tried to do everything the Holy Spirit told him to do. He was eventually found out by the soldiers he had led in the past. They beat him mercilessly and accused him of being a traitor. Somehow—miraculously—God saved this believer from death. Even so, the cost for his service to Jesus was immense. Once he became a follower of Jesus, he was hated and hunted. He gave up, literally, everything to follow Jesus.

Over time, he continued to grow—and he continued to be changed by the power of God. As he told his story, this man explained that God had changed him so completely over the years that he was now a different person. His heart was now different. His perspective was now different. His character was now different. He was being spiritually transformed.

In Philippians 2, the apostle Paul beautifully describes what Christ has done for us so that we might be different. As we consider what Christ has done, we are challenged to think about our own attitudes and behaviors. Paul says clearly that our attitude should be the same as that of Christ Jesus who emptied Himself, humbled Himself, and gave up what was His. Paul essentially says, "This is how it should be with you!"

We follow a Lord who laid down His life. And under His lordship, we lay down our lives too.

In one of his books, A. W. Tozer described someone who would lay down his life—specifically someone who would lay down his life on a cross. Tozer noted that three things would be true about that person:

1. A person on a cross would be facing only one direction;
2. A person on a cross could never turn back;
3. A person on a cross would no longer have any plans of his own.

And while that certainly describes Jesus on the cross, it also ought to describe those who follow Jesus. Jesus told us to "take up our cross daily." This is the way he expects His followers to live. And living that way will mean at least three things for us:

1. It will mean that we will face only one direction. We are committed and passionate in our following of Jesus. And we will not be distracted from that focus.
2. It will mean that we can never turn back—even if the rest of the world does.
3. It will mean that we no longer have any plans of our own. Following Jesus—and following His example— we empty ourselves, we let go of what we think is ours, and we choose a humble, obedient path.

Jesus, of course, is the man on the cross. But His way of living— and His willingness to go to the cross—should define our lives as well.

Lord Jesus, we praise You for what You have done. We praise You for Your willing, obedient sacrifice. We praise You for emptying Yourself, for taking on the form of a servant, and for being obedient even to death on a cross.

Because of what You have done, we are saved.

In Your example, though, we hear a calling for us to take on an attitude—and a way of living—that is just like Yours. As attractive as this calling is—and as clear as this calling is—we are afraid.

We are afraid because we know how costly it will be for us to live that way. Still, we pray that You would empower us to live that way despite the cost.

Lord, we resolve to face in one direction. Lord, we resolve not to turn back. Lord, we resolve to no longer have any plans of our own. We are sold out to You.

Day 46

JUDAS

When Jesus had said this, he was troubled in his spirit and testified, "Truly I tell you, one of you will betray me."

JOHN 13:21

When we first began to tell the stories that we had heard in interviews, we felt the need to be extremely guarded with details. We simply could not bear the thought that we might cause further suffering and persecution if identifying names and places were talked about openly. In those early days, we often changed the names of people and made only vague references to regions and countries.

Even today, many decades later, we often take the same precautions.

It would still be dangerous for many people if specific information and details were to be shared too freely and openly. If some of our stories seem to lack specificity, that may not simply be the result of poor writing—it could reflect our intentional effort to be vague for the sake of the people we are talking about.

We were part of a rather amazing gathering in a small town in East Africa years ago. A donor had arranged a meeting of followers of Jesus from a number of different Muslim-majority countries throughout North Africa and the Middle East. In some cases, these church leaders were able to serve openly in their countries—and in other cases, the church leaders served in complete secrecy. Though gatherings such as this were almost unheard of, we somehow had the opportunity to gather together to study and pray and share stories of what God was doing.

One of the pastors at that gathering served in Iran. He was invited to share about what God was doing in his country. He was told he would have about fifteen minutes to talk. Two hours later, this pastor was still telling us stories about the marvelous and unbelievable activity of God in Iran.

According to the testimony of this pastor, people were coming to faith in Jesus and sharing their faith boldly and openly—and God was blessing their faithfulness. What was most startling was his claim that Muslims were coming to faith in Jesus *through the church in Iran*. It was not merely secret and hidden witness that was bearing fruit; people were being brought into friendship with Jesus openly in believing churches. We were stunned and thrilled to hear that this was happening in Iran.

The testimony of this man included specific details. He was surprisingly open in using the actual names of people and in naming specific places. Normally, there is restraint in what can be shared openly, but this Iranian pastor sensed a freedom to tell the truth openly in this setting. Even as he talked, others at the meeting interrupted him several times and told him to be careful, but he insisted on continuing to tell his story. That day, we heard stories about the activity of God in Iran that we had never heard before. More to the point, we heard stories that day about the activity of God in Iran *that we never could have imagined.*

Two weeks later, after we had all gone our separate ways, we learned that this pastor from Iran had disappeared. His mutilated body was found near his home in Iran. This leader who had been so instrumental in God's work in Iran—and so open about details in our meeting—had been murdered.

At the time, it was unclear exactly what had happened. But five years later, at a meeting in another part of the world, we learned that someone from inside another secret gathering had betrayed this Iranian pastor. Someone who sat at the table with other believers, someone who listened to the stories of God's activity, someone who sang the songs of worship with the gathered group, someone who joined in prayer, someone who claimed to be a follower of Jesus—had betrayed this man of God inside of Iran. And the pastor from Iran paid the ultimate price for that betrayal.

We cannot think about that story without thinking of the story in John 13. Sometimes in the stories of faith there is a character named Judas. And whatever the motive of Judas, the outcome is betrayal.

Sadly, that betrayal often carries a high price.

God, the story of the Iranian pastor takes our breath away. We don't like that story at all. The death of this faithful man seems so . . . heinous. Could things have been handled differently in secret gatherings? Others wonder if perhaps this pastor should have been more reserved in his bold and broad sharing.

But we realize quickly that this is not a story about mistakes and logistics. Rather, this is a story about human hearts. This is a story about how human hearts often become profoundly wicked.

We do not want to be afraid or suspicious or cynical. But we do want to be wise.

Oh God, we don't ever want to be like Judas. And if we ever find ourselves in the presence of a Judas, we pray that we will follow the example of Jesus, loving boldly and broadly while remaining fully aware of the betrayer within His inner circle.

Beyond that, all we can do is trust You. And that is what we will do. Teach us that betrayal is never the end of the story.

Day 47

BURIED WITH CHRIST IN BAPTISM

*Therefore we were buried with him by baptism into death,
in order that, just as Christ was raised from the dead by the
glory of the Father, so we too may walk in newness of life.*

ROMANS 6:4

In our previous story, we talked about the Iranian pastor who
was betrayed and killed for his faith.

There is more to that story . . .

Months after that initial gathering in the small town in East
Africa, another pastor in Iran was preparing to lead worship back at
home. On that day something very special had been planned: dozens of
Muslim Background Believers were preparing to be baptized.

For followers of Jesus who come out of Muslim backgrounds, baptism is a cataclysmic event. It is, we might say, the point of no return.
Before baptism, Muslim family members and friends assume that
people showing interest in Jesus are, perhaps, simply going through a
phase. The assumption is that, once they come to their senses, they will
walk away from Jesus and return to their traditional faith.

With baptism, however, a line is crossed. And it is baptism that
typically opens the door for the fiercest persecution and oppression.
At that point, the persecution and oppression might come from the
government authorities, but it will most likely come from family members—who will be seriously dishonored, embarrassed, and scandalized
by their family member who has decided to become a follower of Jesus.
It is typically baptism that sets severe persecution in motion.

149

On this particular day, thirty-five Muslim-background men were ready to be baptized. They had gathered in an open setting with their church family. This was a public place. These believers could have been following Jesus for several years. They had been trained and taught and mentored. They knew what it would cost them to follow Jesus. And now they had reached the moment when they would cross the line and receive baptism—the point of no return.

Already in the baptismal pool, the pastor was explaining to his church what baptism meant. His wife was holding his cell phone at the time when a call came through. She handed the phone to her husband. In that moment, on the phone, he was told that the mutilated body of the Iranian pastor, who had spoken so boldly at the meeting in East Africa, had been found.

In that moment, he learned what had happened to his dear friend and fellow pastor. At the very moment that he learned of this horrible death . . . he was explaining to those several dozen Muslim Background Believers what it would cost them to be baptized. With tears streaming down his cheeks, he now told them that this cost is very real—and he told them what had happened to his beloved pastor friend.

Significantly, the slain pastor was not merely *his* friend; he had also been the dear friend and mentor of these people waiting to be baptized. It was *their* teacher and friend and pastor who had been killed.

The man in the baptismal pool said to the believers already in line: "Our dear friend is dead. He has been killed for his love for Jesus. Are you ready now to be baptized . . . now that you truly know what this will mean for you?"

Without hesitation, one by one, the believers walked into the water . . . seeking to be baptized . . . knowing exactly what it would mean for them.

The image of baptism suggests new life. Coming up out of the water makes us think of resurrection. But before resurrection can happen, there must be crucifixion.

Understanding this well, those followers of Jesus chose to be, as Scripture says, "buried with Christ by baptism into death."

Baptism into death. It is one thing to read those words as metaphor. It is something altogether different to understand that those words are literally true.

And what are we to make of people who, having come to understand that, choose to be baptized anyway?

Lord God, we wonder sometimes if You are asking too much of us. We wonder sometimes why it isn't a little easier and a little less costly to follow You.

But then we think of the cross, and we feel ashamed about our concerns about cost. And we hear stories of followers today who seem quite willing to embrace the very cost that we try so hard to avoid.

Lord, we confess that we probably haven't really understood baptism. Teach us what it means to be buried with Christ. Teach us what it means to deny ourselves. Teach us what it means to take up our cross.

Lord God, the problem isn't that You ask too much. Instead, the problem is that we are willing to give too little. Forgive us for our lack of courage. Forgive us for being afraid of the cost.

Day 48

THE NEXT GENERATION

My people, hear my instruction; listen to the words from my mouth. I will declare wise sayings; I will speak mysteries from the past—things we have heard and known and that our fathers have passed down to us. We will not hide them from their children, but will tell a future generation the praiseworthy acts of the LORD, his might, and the wonderful works he has performed.

PSALM 78:1–4

For the past two days, we have been reflecting on the story of an Iranian pastor who, first, shared boldly about the activity of God, and then was put to death for his faith.

Just recently, another chapter of his story was written.

The martyrdom of this pastor was a great encouragement to followers of Jesus in Iran and in surrounding countries. His faith was celebrated as an example of faithful devotion and selfless sacrifice. Sometimes we imagine that death and suffering will cause people to walk away from Jesus. In fact, often just the opposite happens. Stories of costly sacrifice spur other believers to stand strong, and to be even more bold.

This pastor who was murdered had a son who was unaware that we had been with his father weeks before his disappearance. He knew, of course, that his father had died, and he knew that his father had been killed for his faith in Jesus. Yet, he had never heard all the stories from the weeks leading up to his father's death, nor had he heard about the impact that his father's death had on multitudes of believers.

Several years ago, we were able to meet the pastor's son. In fact, at a conference together we had the opportunity to interview him in the presence of a large group. As we talked with him in that very public setting, it became apparent to us that he was unaware of significant details about the few weeks preceding his father's martyrdom. It was also clear very quickly that he had little understanding of how much his father's faithfulness had meant to so many believers in persecution globally.

In that very public setting, we were able to share with this young man additional stories about his father. We were able to fill in some gaps and provide details that he had never heard. What was most exciting was telling this young man how faithful his father had been—how his father's faithfulness, even in death, had energized the life of the church for years in Iran—how his father's faithfulness had encouraged the church all around the world.

Right before our eyes, we could see a remarkable change happening in this young man's life. Something holy began to happen even during the interview. The young man was clearly relieved to hear some details about his father that he had never heard before. He was grateful for the legacy that his father had left behind. He was strengthened in his own faith. And he was, assuredly, deeply proud of his father.

We were all encouraged as we celebrated how the faith of a father was passed on to the next generation—and we were deeply humbled that we could be a part of that.

Lord God, You are the God of every generation. You are the God of mothers and fathers. You are the God of children and grandchildren. Thank You for faithful witness that can be shared and passed on. And thank You for opportunities to encounter stories of devotion and faithfulness.

Help us to be eager to tell the stories of Your wonderful works. And help us to be ready to hear the stories that others tell. Change us as we tell and as we hear. Make us, Lord, global citizens within Your kingdom.

OUR FIRST CIRCLE OF INFLUENCE

The next day, John was standing with two of his disciples. When
he saw Jesus passing by, he said, "Look! The Lamb of God!"
Andrew, Simon Peter's brother, was one of the two who heard
John and followed him [Jesus]. He first found his own brother
Simon and told him, "We have found the Messiah" (which
is translated "the Christ"), and he brought Simon to Jesus.

JOHN 1:35–36, 40–42A

Over time we began to notice trends and patterns in our
interviews with believers in persecution. At the beginning, we
followed a list of questions that we had prepared. Quickly, however,
we set those questions aside and simply listened as people told us their
stories. As we listened to (and then transcribed and analyzed) the
interviews, it was not difficult at all to distill certain themes that came
up time and time again.

Among Muslim Background Believers in particular, the theme of
family was dominant. In almost every case, the conversation eventually made its way to family—and specifically to the relationship the
believer had with his or her parents. Often, that relationship was not
good at all.

In fact, we discovered that many of these believers had become
followers of Jesus hoping that their decision to follow Jesus would actually inflict pain on their parents, especially on their fathers. Having

experienced the damage that the father had sometimes inflicted on the family, choosing to follow Jesus was a way to "pay him back."

In other cases, followers of Jesus had waited to declare their faith in Jesus until their parents (especially their father) had died. It was as if the death of the father set them free to act on their commitment.

In still other situations, we met deeply committed followers of Jesus *who had never told their parents that they were believers!*

The dynamic of family relationships is perhaps always complicated—but it seemed to be especially complicated for the people we were interviewing. We were troubled to learn that hatred for family was often a significant motivational element in the stories of conversion that we were hearing.

When we suggested that these believers should share their faith in Jesus with their families, they were generally incredulous. We went even further and suggested that their relationship with Jesus should lead them to go to their family, to share with their family, and to love their family. Hearing that, many of these believers told us that such behavior would be impossible—that it was simply too much to ask. Some even said to us that—if that was required—they would not be able to follow Jesus any longer. Some were quite direct: "I simply cannot do that! I simply will not do that!"

In processing these difficult and troubling conversations, we recognized how very different the situation was in China, Russia, and India. In those places, believers tend to eagerly embrace the opportunity to share with family members. As a result, the growth of the church in those areas is often explosive.

Our closest circles of influence will be the most natural place to share our faith—and in China, Russia, and India that can be done. Often, our closest circle of influence is family. Among Muslim Background Believers, however, family may not be seen as the first place to share faith—instead, family will often be the most dangerous place for a believer to share.

When Andrew met Jesus, he immediately found his brother (Simon Peter) and told him what had happened. Andrew didn't look for a stranger; he looked for the person who was closest to him. Andrew introduced his brother to Jesus—and that made possible a life-long and life-changing friendship with Jesus.

It is tragic when believers are not able to follow Andrew's example. The unwillingness or the inability to share faith in family settings will greatly inhibit the spread of the faith.

God, we have a hard time understanding the family dynamics that define life for many people around the world. We cannot imagine how people can choose to follow Jesus against the will of their parents. We know better than simply to suggest that those people should act courageously. Though that might be important, our hearts hurt when we think about the pressure, the judgment, and even the violence that might follow the decision to follow Jesus.

And yet, You continue to call us to follow You. You call us to follow You when our families approve, and when they do not. Help us all to navigate these relationships with humility, grace, kindness, respect—and, yes, ultimately with courage.

Help us to love our families. But even as we love our families, help us to live in radical submission to You.

Day 50

SENT INTO THE STORM

On that day, when evening had come, he told them, "Let's cross over to the other side of the sea." So they left the crowd and took him along since he was in the boat. And other boats were with him. A great windstorm arose, and the waves were breaking over the boat, so that the boat was already being swamped.

MARK 4:35–37

When we told people in the States about our struggles on the mission field, there was often a measure of confusion. When we asked what they were thinking, they told us that they had always assumed that people who went to serve overseas would somehow be "protected" from suffering. They suggested that people who are already sacrificing for Jesus should somehow be exempt from additional loss and heartache. People admitted that they had no real reason to hold this view—except that it seemed "fair" to them.

This turned out to be a profound lesson for us. Somewhat related was an attitude toward persecution that we encountered later: the mistaken idea that persecution happened when a follower of Jesus *did something wrong*. Repeatedly, we heard persecution described as a problem to be avoided, an unfortunate happening that was unnecessary, and something that simply could not be a part of God's plan. The underlying idea was that if we did things "right," things would always work out. More broadly, it was believed that if followers of Jesus were faithful and obedient, they would be protected from suffering and sacrifice.

Our own experience with suffering—and our conversations with hundreds of persecuted believers—told us something quite different. We came to understand that many of the storms that come to Jesus' followers—including, of course, the storm of persecution—come specifically *because* followers of Jesus are living out their faith boldly and obediently!

Suffering comes, in some cases, not because we are doing something wrong—but precisely because we are doing something right!

Indeed, sometimes we encounter storms of our own choosing. In some cases, our struggles grow directly out of our disobedience to God. But only sometimes . . .

At other times, the storms are a direct result of doing exactly what Jesus has asked us to do.

The familiar story that we read in Mark 4:35–41 is a favorite that highlights the power of Jesus over the forces of nature as well as His deep love for those who follow Him. Simply hearing the words that Jesus speaks to the wind and the sea reminds us of His marvelous strength: "Silence! Be still!" Like the disciples in the story, we marvel: "Who then is this? Even the wind and the sea obey him!"

But this story also helps us understand the storms of life. Again, our normal presumption is that storms come because we have done something wrong. It is crucial to notice, however, that the disciples (in Mark 4:35–41) *are led into the storm by Jesus*!

It is Jesus who tells them to get into the boat.

The storm that the disciples encounter is not caused by their disobedience or by their failure or by their mistakes. In fact, they find themselves in a storm *specifically because of their obedience.* They have done what Jesus has asked them to do. Jesus says to them quite simply, "Let's cross over to the other side of the sea."

And the disciples obediently respond by climbing into the boat.

There is clearly no special exemption for those who obey. In fact, sometimes the storms come—and sometimes persecution happens—and sometimes losses occur—*because* of our obedience.

Lord God, we don't care much for storms. We would prefer simply to avoid them. In fact, our normal presumption is that it is Your job to keep storms away from us.

How strange, though, to be told that You use storms for Your purposes! How unbelievable to be told that You sometimes send storms! And how stunning to realize that sometimes You send Your children into storms!

Teach us to trust Your ways even when we do not understand Your ways. Teach us that some storms may come because we are being faithful and obedient to You.

We have much to learn about Your unusual ways. We never imagined that You would send us into storms. But right here—in the middle of the storm—we see that even the wind and the waves obey You.

Day 51

WHEN THE WORLD COMES TO US

> *"How is it that each of us can hear them in our own*
> *native language? Parthians, Medes, Elamites; those who*
> *live in Mesopotamia, in Judea and Cappadocia, Pontus*
> *and Asia, Phrygia and Pamphylia, Egypt and the parts*
> *of Libya near Cyrene; visitors from Rome (both Jews and*
> *converts), Cretans and Arabs—we hear them declaring*
> *the magnificent acts of God in our own tongues."*
>
> ACTS 2:8–11

Within one single zip code in the United States . . . one hundred eighty languages are spoken.

The zip code is 11372. The neighborhood, which has a population of over 100,000 people, is called Jackson Heights, and is in the borough of Queens in New York City.

The whole world, it seems, has come to Jackson Heights.

If someone were to be mysteriously transported into the heart of this neighborhood without knowing exactly where they were, it would be quite difficult to figure out the location using only sights, smells, and sounds. If asked about the location, the first guess would likely be another country. With one hundred eighty languages being spoken, it might take a long time even to hear someone speaking English.

This world community . . . is in our own country. This neighborhood can be reached easily by public transit. Visiting there requires no passport and no special immunizations. For those who live on the East Coast, a visit there does not even require a time change.

Clearly, followers of Jesus are called to go to the ends of the earth to share in God's work. But how marvelous that God would find a way to bring the world to us at the very same time!

Not every city is like Jackson Heights, of course. Your city, for example, might not look anything like Jackson Heights. Even so, many of our cities and neighborhoods are populated with people who come from many different places and with people who speak different languages. Sometimes these people are hard to see and hard to find. If we pay careful attention, however, and if we pray for the kind of insight that comes from God, we will be drawn to the peoples of the earth who have come to live very close to us.

For followers of Jesus, we should see the presence of these people as a precious gift from God. How amazing that God would give us an opportunity to touch the world for Jesus—often without even leaving our own neighborhood!

Yes, we are called to go to the world. But sometimes, in His grace, God brings the world to us.

If you ever want to see the whole world, take a trip to Jackson Heights.

Or simply take a walk around your own neighborhood. You might be quite surprised by what you see!

Lord God, You have the world on Your heart. And You call us to love the world. You call us to go to the world.

Sometimes, however, You bring the world to us! Help us to see this as a holy opportunity. Help us to see the presence of the world in our midst as one more way that we can share Jesus. Help us not to miss opportunities that are present and close by in our own neighborhood and city.

Day 52

BUILDING BRIDGES WITH PEOPLE

Then Levi hosted a grand banquet for him [Jesus]
at his house. Now there was a large crowd of tax
collectors and others who were guests with them.

LUKE 5:29

As we think about God's call to go to the Nations, we also think about the people in our own towns and neighborhoods who need to hear about Jesus. We are compelled not simply to care about them, but also to find ways to share Jesus with them. Sometimes the challenge is the actual telling of our story—but often the challenge is simply finding points of connection with people. As individual followers of Jesus and as churches of gathered believers, we will intentionally seek ways to build bridges with people so that Jesus might be shared.

In Matthew 5, we glimpse an example of bridge-building. Levi has just been invited to follow Jesus. In response to Jesus' call, Levi has left his work behind and has started walking with Jesus. At that point, he hosts a grand banquet and invites people who do not yet know Jesus. According to the text, Jesus attends the banquet as well. Clearly, Levi's intention is to find some way to connect his friends and coworkers with Jesus. Levi is interested in something more than simply hosting a party; his invitation to his friends has an evangelistic purpose.

In the same way, we look for ways to share our faith. The bridges that we seek to build come in all shapes and sizes. The spiritual needs present in our communities are so great that we are compelled to be creative and bold in our search for connections.

In some communities, there is a desperate need for people to teach English. You might be aware of needs in your city that relate to housing or food. In some places, children and youth need tutoring. Some families struggle to find resources for disabled children. Some communities have significant medical or dental needs. Sometimes the need is simply friendship, or perhaps a group where a sense of belonging can be found. We can often find people who need help because of natural disasters. People in care facilities and hospitals are desperate for visits. We could simply open our homes and practice the spiritual gift of hospitality.

There is simply no limit to the possibilities of how we can care for people and address very real needs. And as we serve in this way, we make possible the sharing of our faith.

As we seek ways to serve and share, we should pray first and simply ask that God would bring the needs of our community to mind. Once we pray, we should be ready to act on whatever needs God brings to our attention. We obviously want to help people; that pull to ministry is simply part of who we are as followers of Jesus. But as we help, we have another goal in mind. We want every person in the world to have the opportunity to hear about Jesus. Our ministries of help and compassion build bridges that make that opportunity possible.

All over the world, followers of Jesus look for ways to connect with people so that the story of Jesus might be shared. That is not simply a "mission strategy" for those who serve overseas. That is the calling of every follower of Jesus—and the calling of every church.

We will do whatever it takes to build friendship with people—in the hope that the story of Jesus can be shared. Jesus often used the opportunity of a shared meal to introduce others to His coming kingdom. Opening your home to the Nations, sharing a meal with them, is one of the most Jesus-like ministries you can emulate.

God, give us vision to see how exactly we might meet the needs of the people who live around us. As we address those very real needs, give us opportunities to build genuine friendships. And from the beginning, give us the courage to tell them about Jesus.

Help us to be creative and sensitive and compassionate as we look at our cities and neighborhoods. Help us to remember that Your grace is meant to be shared. Help us to remember that meeting needs is a wonderful way to open a door where sharing Jesus is possible. Like Levi, teach us to be creative in finding ways to introduce people to You. Allow our homes, Lord, to become a crossroad where strangers become family.

Day 53

OVERCOMING OUR FEAR

*Then David said to his son Solomon, "Be strong and
courageous, and do the work. Don't be afraid or
discouraged, for the LORD God, my God, is with you."*

1 CHRONICLES 28:20A

Fear can be devastating.

Whether we are talking about the fear that surfaces when
persecution comes—the fear that we feel when it's time to share our
faith—the fear that weakens our resolve—the fear that makes it difficult for us to obey . . . most of us struggle mightily with fear at some
level.

While we are encouraged to trust God, and believe that He is at
work—and we are invited to live lives of confident joy . . . we often
struggle and doubt. We sometimes even quit.

*What if something happens? What if this doesn't work out? What if
we fail? Or what if we succeed? What if we cannot handle this? What if
we share with people and they refuse to listen? What if our ministry doesn't
work? What if we get in trouble? What if we're not up to the task? What if
God lets us down? What if we're rejected? What if we get hurt? What if we
run out of money? What if we make a stupid mistake? What if other people
judge us? What if we're not strong enough?*

What if . . . ?

And those questions are just the beginning! I'm sure you could add hundreds of similar questions to the list. And behind every one of those questions is fear. And if we give in to fear, we will end up doing nothing.

The persecuted followers of Jesus that we have talked with often admitted that they, too, were afraid. In some cases, their fear never disappeared. Still—somehow—they seemed to find ways to move forward even with their fear. They did not necessarily overcome their fear—but they found a way to act despite it.

In the Bible, God is forever saying, "Do not be afraid!" He says that not because the threats are not real, but because He is wise and strong. He says that not because we are always going to get it right, but because He can work with whatever we offer. He says that not because we are competent and strong, but because He is.

God would surely prefer that we not be afraid—but in His grace, He calls us to obedience even when we are.

There is a lot to be said for being afraid, and taking the next step anyway. Maybe when we do that—and when we see what God can do—fear gradually loses its power over us.

The fact that God is with us makes all the difference in the world.

God, give us courage. We are often a fearful people. We are afraid of serving, going, giving, sharing, loving. Despite Your strength, we are afraid that we are not good enough, strong enough, pure enough, competent enough. Our fear can be debilitating—and it can keep us from obedience.

Forgive us for being fearful people.

Teach us not to be afraid. Even more, teach us that, even if we are afraid, You can still use us. Call us forward and give us the courage that we need to take the next step.

Day 54

THE LONG VIEW

*And he said, "With what can we compare the kingdom of
God, or what parable can we use to describe it? It's like a
mustard seed that, when sown upon the soil, is the smallest of
all the seeds on the ground. And when sown, it comes up and
grows taller than all the garden plants, and produces large
branches, so that the birds of the sky can nest in its shade."*

MARK 4:30–32

Throughout our ministry, one of our greatest struggles came
from our inability to identify good results, measurable fruit,
or typical markers of success. We were never interested in building
ourselves up; we simply wanted to know that all of our hard work was
producing some good result. And in many seasons of our life, there was
simply nothing to point to.

We had friends who served overseas who would come home to the
States periodically and tell wonderful stories of church planting movements and visible evidence of the activity of God's Spirit. Churches in
the States were justifiably thrilled at such stories; people were deeply
encouraged to know that God was at work, and that overseas workers
were able to produce such amazing fruit.

In contrast, however, we generally had a different story to tell.
We, too, came home and visited churches. We, too, could tell stories
of God's activity. But we were unable to paint pictures of productive
ministry and measurable growth. (In some seasons, we were happy to

be able to come home and simply tell people that there were followers of Jesus in the countries where we were serving who were still alive!)

How long will you persevere in ministry without evidence of success? How long are you willing to press on when there seems to be almost nothing to count or measure? How willing are you to be faithful to God's call when it seems that you are serving in a dry place where growing fruit seems almost impossible?

And how long will you share Jesus with your neighbor before you decide that it's hopeless? How long will you invest in a hard place in your community when it seems that nothing much is happening? How much money will your church spend in a ministry that seems to be "of God," but doesn't seem to be bearing fruit?

These are hard questions, and sometimes strategic decisions require that we find the best way to use the resources that God has provided. Sometimes, it is time to walk away from a ministry opportunity.

In every case, though, faithfulness to the call of God is the highest concern. When we can point to measurable results—and when we cannot—we choose to be faithful.

It could be that we will be asked to invest years of our lives in a ministry that seems to be completely unsuccessful. In His Great Commission, Jesus commands us to go to ALL of the world's peoples, not just to those who are quickly responsive or more cost-effective.

And it could be that, even if we can point to no fruit, the mustard seed is growing the whole time. We would be wise to take the long view and simply leave the results in God's hands.

What we are responsible for is . . . our faithfulness.

We have a hard time, Lord, seeing what is happening. We have a hard time seeing what You are doing. We are drawn to things that we can count and measure and quantify. But so much of Your work doesn't lend itself to those categories. Your work is often silent and slow and sudden. One day there is only a seed in the ground; it appears that nothing is happening. Then one day, there is a tree!

Help us to wait. Help us to endure. Help us to remain faithful. Help us to leave the results that we can see and the results that we cannot see in Your capable hands.

Day 55

THE PROBLEM WITH BOLD CLAIMS

*I proclaimed a fast by the Ahava River, so that we might humble
ourselves before our God and ask him for a safe journey for
us, our dependents, and all our possessions. I did this because
I was ashamed to ask the king for infantry and cavalry to
protect us from enemies during the journey, since we had
told him, "The hand of our God is gracious to all who seek
him, but his fierce anger is against all who abandon him."*

EZRA 8:21–22

We decided early on that we wanted whatever God wanted. In fact, we made it a point to tell God that we would be obedient without conditions. Often, we found ourselves saying "Yes" to God even before we knew exactly what we were saying "Yes" to! The details didn't really matter all that much to us; we were committed to God's call—regardless of the details.

In taking that approach, we are often reminded of the Old Testament character of Ezra. His responsibility was to lead God's people back to Jerusalem after a time of exile. In his preparations, Ezra had made bold claims about God's ability to protect His people and to provide for their needs. When it was time to start the journey back to Jerusalem, however, Ezra and the people began to sense how dangerous the journey would be. In fact, the danger was so great that Ezra wanted very much to seek help from the king. And it is likely that the king would have provided soldiers to protect Ezra and his people.

But Ezra had already made bold claims about God's ability to provide.

Ezra had already laid it on the line. Even before he knew exactly how things might play out, Ezra had declared his absolute allegiance to God. And because of that, he was ashamed to ask the king for soldiers and horsemen (Ezra 8:22).

Ezra was bound by his bold claims!

In our lives, our bold claims boxed us in too. We had already affirmed our willingness to obey God—no matter what He would ask. We had already said "Yes"—not knowing exactly where God might lead. Just like Ezra, we were bound by our bold claims.

And we never regretted those claims. In fact, it may be that those bold claims made obedience simpler. We had already placed our lives in the hands of God—and we were determined to follow through and trust Him.

To put it another way, our commitment was to God—not to a specific task that He might put before us. And because we were absolutely committed to God, we were ready to do anything that He would ask.

We ended up being grateful for our bold claims. Having declared our allegiance to God, obedience was simply a matter of following through. Yet it was a good thing that our obedience was in place before we heard of a place called Somalia! By then it was too late to back out and renegotiate our "contract" with God.

*God of Power and Grace, You hear every word we say.
Even more, You know every thought we think. And You
know when our words and our thoughts reflect what is
truly in our hearts—and You know when they don't.*

*Lord God, we often make bold claims about Your power and Your
wisdom and Your grace. We say out loud that You are able, that You
know what is best, and that we will do whatever it is that You ask.*

*And those bold claims sometimes reveal us to be liars. Forgive us
for failing to live lives that truly reflect what we say about You.
Help us to be like Ezra—actually ashamed to back down because of
what we have already said. Give us the courage to make even bolder
claims about You and about our commitment to You. Then help us
to live out those claims with integrity and consistency and courage.*

Day 56

GOING WITH NO GUARANTEES

*Now all the believers were together and held all things
in common. They sold their possessions and property and
distributed the proceeds to all, as any had need.*

ACTS 2:44–45

When a Russian pastor was arrested and sent to prison, his wife and children were sent far away to Siberia. The pastor's family barely survived in a dilapidated cabin. They had very little food.

One evening, as this mother and her three young children ate their last crust of bread and had their last sip of tea, the children cried, "Mama, where's Daddy?" "Mama, I'm hungry." "Mama, I'm cold and scared." "Mama, are we going to die?"

Hardly believing it herself, she answered: "God knows where we are, and God will take care of us. Children, we have taught you all of your lives to trust God. Now it is time to trust Him."

Thirty kilometers away, God woke up a deacon who was part of a church that this pastor's family knew nothing about. In the middle of the night, this man sensed a very clear word from God. He was told: "Get out of bed. Harness your horse. Hitch the horse to the sled. Load up all the extra vegetables that the church has harvested and the meat and other food that has been collected. Take it to the pastor's family living outside the village. They are hungry!"

The man argued, "But, Lord, I can't do that! It is freezing outside. My horse might freeze. I might freeze."

But the Holy Spirit said clearly, "You must go! The pastor's family is in trouble!"

Again, the man argued, "Lord, You know that there are wolves. They could eat my horse. And if they do, then they will eat me. I will never make it back."

At that point, the Spirit responded, "You don't have to come back. You just have to go."

So the man went.

When he knocked on the door of that rickety cabin in the pre-dawn hours the next morning, the banging on the door terrified the pastor's family. But imagine the joy and amazement when they fearfully opened the door to find this faithful follower of Jesus delivering food from one part of the body of Christ to another part!

The man said, "God wants us to give you this. When this food is gone, we will bring more."

Most of us would prefer to minimize our risk when we decide to obey God's call. And even if we are willing to bear some risk, we want very much to know that things will work out well. We might pore over the Great Commission searching for a hint of a guarantee. We want so much to find some assurance that, if we indeed go, at least we can be promised that we will come back!

But there is no guarantee . . . other than the guarantee that Jesus Himself will be with us.

We don't have to come back . . . but we do have to go.

*Father, if we fail to go to others when they are in need, do we
have any right to expect help when our needs are unmet?*

*Lord, compel us to go even though there is no promise
that we will even survive to return to our safe place.*

Day 57

CRUCIFIXION OF THE WILL

*He went a little farther, fell to the ground, and prayed that if
it were possible, the hour might pass from him. And he said,
"Abba, Father! All things are possible for you. Take this cup away
from me. Nevertheless, not what I will, but what you will."*

MARK 14:35–36

A common refrain echoed throughout dozens of testimonies
from persecuted believers across the former Soviet Union.
In the face of intense pressure and severe persecution, these believers
continued in their faithful obedience to God. Whether they lived or
died—whether they were intimidated or locked in prison—whether
they were subject to physical threats or psychological torture—they
still maintained their trust in God and their desire to remain true to
God's call.

How was this possible?

Our questions to them sounded something like this: *How did you
learn to live like this? How did you learn to die like that?*

In answer to those questions, a believer in Ukraine offered this
response:

> I remember the day like it was yesterday. My father put his
> arms around me and my sister and my brother and sat us
> down for a talk. My Mama was crying so I knew something
> was wrong. Papa said, "Children, you know that I am
> the pastor of our church. That's what God has called me to

179

do—to tell others about Him. I have learned that the com-
munist authorities will arrest me tomorrow. They will put me
in prison because they want me to stop preaching about Jesus.
But I cannot stop preaching about Jesus; I must obey God. I
will miss you very much, but I will trust God to watch over
you while I am gone."

He hugged us tightly. Then my father said, "All around
our country, the authorities are rounding up followers of Jesus
and demanding that they deny their faith. Sometimes, when
the believers refuse to deny their faith, the authorities will
punish their families—and sometimes even put the family
members to death. I don't want that to happen to our family.
However (and here he paused and made eye contact with
each one of us), if I am in prison and I hear that my wife and
my children have been put to death for their faith in Jesus, I
will be the most proud man in that prison."

We were stunned by his words. Never in our church growing up, never in our theological training, never in our mission preparation had we encountered commitment at that level. We had never been told or taught that a father should value his faith over his family. We had never been encouraged to live out that kind of sacrifice.

Even so, we quickly realized that sacrifice of that magnitude was at the heart of the biblical story of Jesus. In the garden, just before His crucifixion, Jesus asked the Father to take "this cup" away. The cup is a biblical image for divinely-appointed suffering and the image clearly refers to the cross.

But Jesus' heartfelt request was followed by this crucial word: "Nevertheless, not what I will, but what You will."

Jesus relinquished His will into His Father's hands; He submitted completely to what His Father desired.

And we are expected to do the same. This is what we must pray if we are to be faithful and obedient: "Father, Your will be done!" When we pray this prayer, we are saying that God can do what we cannot do. When we pray this prayer, we are saying that, even though we might be uncertain about the next step, we are utterly certain about God. When we pray this prayer, we are removing our will from the conversation and placing our very lives in the hands of God. Often we are quick to pray the first half of that prayer, asking God to rescue us. That's a good prayer. Yet we must pray both halves of the prayer of Jesus asking that the Father's will be done.

This is total surrender—and total surrender is our highest calling and our greatest privilege. The tighter we cling to what we have—the tighter we cling to our plans, our intentions, our expectations, our needs, our demands—the less chance there is that we will ever experience the joy and life that God has prepared for those who truly trust Him.

Heavenly Father, we struggle with submission. It is simply not in our nature to submit—even to You. Actually, it is not in our nature to submit—especially to You! We never know what You might ask or expect or demand. You seem to know what we are least willing to give up. And that is often the very thing You ask of us.

So here is the truth: we are perfectly happy to follow Your will . . . as long as Your will lines up with what we want.

But we know full well that You will not settle for that. And we know full well that we do not really want that either. Truly, Your will captivates and captures us. Your will sometimes scares us to death, but it captivates and captures us just the same. In our hearts—in our best moments—we sincerely want what You want. So we relinquish our will to You. We relinquish to You our will . . . because it already belongs to You. We trust You with our very lives.

Day 58

AN AUDIENCE OF ONE

*Very early in the morning, while it was still dark, he got up,
went out, and made his way to a deserted place; and there he
was praying. Simon and his companions searched for him, and
when they found him they said, "Everyone's looking for you."
And he said to them, "Let's go on to the neighboring villages
so that I may preach there too. This is why I have come."*

MARK 1:35–38

Persecuted believers in China taught us about the immense cost of speaking the basic affirmation of our faith. Just to say the words "Jesus is Lord" places a Chinese believer in clear and costly opposition to an authoritarian government that will allow no rival. To say that Jesus is Lord is to say, at the very same time, that the government is not Lord. And to acquiesce to the government's claim of authority would prevent a citizen from truly following Jesus as Lord.

Throughout the world—but highlighted in China—a choice is demanded. If Jesus is Lord, no one else is. There is no middle ground.

According to the persecuted believers in China that we interviewed, the government's long-standing opposition to religion has little to do with faith, and everything to do with control. The government is fully aware that someone who is committed to Jesus will not be easy to control. A follower of Jesus will answer to a higher authority, and they will side with Jesus every time there is a conflict. Any faith that calls for obedience to God is a threat to the government—and, therefore, cannot be tolerated. The faith of believers strikes at the heart of government's power.

The perspective of the Chinese believers invites us to consider who or what we answer to.

The perspective of the Chinese believers challenges us to think about what authority is binding on our lives.

Jesus Himself faced the same dilemma. In Mark 1, the disciples track Jesus down early in the morning after He has gotten up early to pray. In the midst of a very successful season of ministry, the disciples tell Jesus that everyone is looking for Him. The clear implication is that Jesus should respond to the immediate needs of the crowd—and that He should continue with the ministry that had already been started.

Jesus, however, says that He is going to go someplace else. Guided by His time with the Father, Jesus knows exactly what He should do and where He should go. He does not give in to the counsel of the disciples or to the needs of the people. Jesus answers only to His Father. He knows that only the Father can give guidance and direction. The demands of the Father control Jesus' heart and mind. The Father is His only audience, the only one He desires to please.

This is the challenge for each one of us. Who will we please? Whose expectations will we fulfill? Whose demands will get our attention? Who will be our audience? To whom will we answer?

In simplest terms, we have an audience of One. God's opinion is the only one that matters.

God, we want to believe that we can please you AND that we can please everyone else at the same time. Yes, we realize how silly that sounds, yet that is where we normally live. What's more, because the demands of people are often louder than Your voice, we tend to please people at the expense of pleasing You. Forgive us, Father.

You matter supremely. What You want holds sway over us. What You think matters. Still, we struggle to live in the light of that simple truth. So set us free to please You. Set us free to care only about what You desire. Deliver us from our need to be honored and appreciated and understood by others.

God, this is going to be hard for us—but it is our desire to please You alone.

Day 59

STAYING PUT

*For the Lord has said to me, "Go, post a lookout; let him
report what he sees. When he sees riders—pairs of horsemen,
riders on donkeys, riders on camels—he must pay close
attention." Then the lookout reported, "Lord, I stand on
the watchtower all day, and I stay at my post all night."*

ISAIAH 21:6–8

Over the years, there were many opportunities to walk away
from our call.

The problem was not merely our own feelings of inadequacy.
What disturbed us even more was the staggering level of need. What
we encountered almost daily was crushing and crippling suffering. And
many days it simply seemed to be too much.

Even when we discovered a way to address specific (and sometimes
substantial) needs, we almost immediately encountered additional
needs that we hadn't even noticed before. One day, we talked with a
bent-over, shriveled-up woman. "Tell us what you need most," we said.
"What can we do for you right now?" She looked ancient, but she may
have only been in her forties if we understood correctly the story that
she told:

> *I grew up in a village many days walk from here. My father
> was a nomad who raised cattle and sheep. I married a camel
> herder who had a similar kind of life. He was a good man;
> together we had a good life and four children. The war came*

186

and the militia marched through our village, stealing or slaughtering most of our animals. When my husband tried to stop them from taking our last camel, militia men beat him, and then they put a gun to his head. They killed him.

I worked hard to care for my children after my husband was killed, but the drought came. When my neighbors left for the city, some of them gave me what they couldn't carry with them. So I tried to make do . . . but there wasn't enough. My oldest boy got sick and died. When the last of our food was almost gone, my children and I began walking. I hoped that life would be better here in the city. But it is not better—it is harder. Men with guns are everywhere. They assaulted me and beat me. They took my older daughters. I only have this little one left. There is no work for a woman alone. I don't know how I will take care of her. I know no one in this place. But I don't have anywhere else to go.

We learned that simply listening to this woman was something important that we could offer. But the need that she expressed in her story broke our hearts. We were absolutely committed to God's call—but we still wondered how long we could stay in the presence of such suffering.

In Isaiah 21, we meet a lookout, a watchman who has been told to stay at his post . . . and watch. His task is simply to report what he sees. His assignment doesn't seem all that dangerous, but it is tedious. Most days, nothing happens. There is generally nothing to report.

But one day something is different (v. 9). One day, something happens. Now, the lookout has a message that must be passed on to others. And the watchman speaks to the people and tells them what has happened. This is a dramatic moment, but a moment that comes after a long, long time of just watching and waiting.

Still, the watchman has been true to his task. He has remained faithful. He has not left his post.

In fact, the measure of the watchman's life can be summed up in this one claim: "Lord, I stand on the watchtower all day, and I stay at my post all night" (Isa. 21:8).

Our highest hope is that we will one day be able to say that we did exactly what our Lord called us to do. No more than that. And certainly no less than that. Whatever our assignment, we are wise to choose to be faithful to our assignment.

It is easy to tell the Potter how we might be best used. It is easy to tell the Potter that we should be in some other place. But we are not the Potter; we are the clay.

So we simply say: "I will not walk away. I will be faithful with my assignment. I will stay at my post."

Creator God, we belong to You. You are free to use us however You see fit. Sometimes it is Your purpose that we simply show up. In response to that purpose, we accept our assignment gladly, joyfully, and without complaint. We trust You—and we long to trust You more.

You are the Potter. We are the clay. Mold us and make us. Have Your way. Despite our opinions and preferences—and in the face of the disappointment and discouragement that we sometimes feel—we choose not to question You and Your ways. Instead, when we wake up each morning, let our first thought be this: we belong to you! That truth, that identity, that gift—defines all that we are and all that we do.

Day 60

ORDINARY SUFFERING

Now we have this treasure in clay jars, so that this extraordinary power may be from God and not from us. We are afflicted in every way but not crushed; we are perplexed but not in despair; we are persecuted but not abandoned; we are struck down but not destroyed. We always carry the death of Jesus in our body, so that the life of Jesus may also be displayed in our body.

2 CORINTHIANS 4:7–10

Every story that we hear is different. But at the same time, in some ways, every story sounds the same.

In a small rural village in Africa, we invited a husband and wife to tell us their stories. As followers of Jesus in a dangerous environment, this couple had endured great suffering. Even though their country is officially an "open" country (meaning that following Jesus is technically "allowed"), there is nevertheless intense negative pressure from those who hold power in the villages and towns.

One at a time, they each told us their stories.

Despite growing up in a non-Christian faith tradition, the man somehow heard about Jesus. He was immediately drawn to the gospel. He told us about the intense judgment of his family, periods of rejection, and grievous persecution from his father. For some reason, this man was able to cling to his new faith in Jesus—despite the pressure of his family. The man shared that many years later several of his family members had started to follow Jesus too. As he continued his story, we heard about times spent in jail. When we asked him if he felt that he had suffered for Jesus, the man paused for a long time. Finally, he answered the question, but he completely reshaped what we had asked. Instead of talking about suffering, he talked about the joy that Jesus gives him. He spoke of the privilege it is to belong to Jesus.

Then it was time for his wife to tell her story. She, too, had grown up in a different faith tradition. Somehow she also had heard about Jesus, and she gave her life to Him. Not surprisingly, there was the requisite rejection from her family. There was also her faithfulness in staying true to her commitment to Jesus. More recently, she shared, she has experienced ugly abuse from the community as she attempts to provide a school for children in the village. Because she does not hold to the faith of the majority, she is seen as a threat and she is opposed at every turn. With a gentle smile, she spoke only of the joy of living with Jesus. She mentioned repeatedly His provision and care. When asked about her suffering, she too shifted the question and refused to acknowledge that there was anything unusual or extraordinary about the hard things in her life.

Everything we heard from these two was so matter of fact. To us, it sounded like a Bible story. To these two followers of Jesus, it sounded just like ordinary life as a follower of Jesus.

When we asked how we could pray for them, they both immediately asked that we would pray that they would have the courage to live truthful lives. That was the actual word they used: *truthful*. What they wanted was to live lives that matched their faith. They also asked us to pray that God would give them the courage to share their faith.

It didn't even dawn on us until much later that they never asked that we pray that they would be set free from their suffering for Jesus.

In fact, they saw their suffering as simply an ordinary part of following Jesus. It never crossed their minds to imagine that an ordinary part of following Jesus could be removed.

God, teach us about expectations. Teach us to consider our expectations of what we deserve, our expectations about what we feel that we have earned because of our willingness to follow You, and our expectations about what is ordinary and unsurprising. Give us a new and fresh way of looking at things.

Change our focus so that we might see Your provision and care instead of our pain and loss. Help us to be more matter-of-fact about the nature of this life with You.

SMALL THINGS

"For who despises the day of small things?"
ZECHARIAH 4:10A

✝ Even though we knew that it wasn't true, we struggled to shake the expectation about how things would work out if we were faithful, if we prayed hard enough, and if we worked diligently. We simply assumed that if we did those things, we would experience success in ministry.

We also had our own pre-conceived definition of what "success" would look like: people coming to faith in Christ, spiritual growth that could be quantified, the birth of new churches—and the kinds of things that are easy to see and measure.

We were quite surprised to discover that those kinds of results rarely came our way. While our times of ministry in Malawi and in the Transkei were fruitful, our time serving in Somalia was completely different. Rarely could we point to anything that looked successful at all. We were doing some good things, to be sure. People were being fed and cared for. But the spiritual side of things looked like complete failure to us.

Frankly, that was hard to take. After all, we were being faithful. We were praying hard. And we were working diligently. We were doing everything we knew to do. Even so, much of the time, it seemed that nothing was happening.

Looking back, however, we can see so many ways that God was at work, so many small things that mattered, so many things that we never even noticed at the time.

In 538 BC, King Cyrus (who had recently conquered Babylon) issued a decree that allowed the Jews to return to Jerusalem to rebuild the temple. The Jews had been in exile—and they were now being allowed to come home. Led by Zerubbabel, about fifty thousand Jews headed home. What they discovered when they got there was devastating. Their beloved temple, of course, had been completely destroyed. In fact, almost everything had been destroyed. Resolute—they started building.

About two years later, they had completed the foundation for the new temple. When enemies saw what was happening, they opposed the work and it ground to a halt. Haggai and Zechariah were prophets who lived at that time—and they encouraged God's people to get back to work. These prophets were certainly interested in spiritual renewal, but they focused their attention on encouraging the people to start building again.

In Zechariah 4, the prophet assures the people that Zerubbabel will indeed finish the work—and he tells them that this success will be a sign of God's presence among them.

And then Zerubbabel asks an interesting question: "Who despises the day of small things?"

Who despises the day of small things?

Actually, we all do! We are not often drawn to small things. Especially when it comes to our service, we are not drawn to small things. Instead, we want big things. We want to see thousands come to Christ. We want revival. We want bold and dramatic seasons of God's activity. We want missionaries who can come back to the States with stories of great church planting movements. Generally, we are not all that interested in small things—and we are certainly not interested in failure.

But even though they don't look like much, small things suggest beginnings. Small things are what God often starts with.

A prayer. A couple of people gathered in a room. A mustard seed. A child. One simple act of kindness. An open door. One person with a sincere desire to follow Jesus. Small things that God can use to build His kingdom. One family with a sincere desire to follow Jesus.

There is a wonder in small things. Sometimes, small things can be hard to see; we tend not even to notice them. But with the right kind of vision, we can see the small things that are happening all around us. Those small things are clear evidence that God is at work.

God of Possibility, forgive us for being so easily impressed with the big and the beautiful and the flashy. You seem much more interested in things of no account. You seem much more interested in people of no account. Honestly, so much of what we see looks like failure to us. We are almost certain that it will all amount to nothing. But our faulty assessment ignores Your power and belittles Your startling creativity.

Set us free to believe. Set us free to believe You. Set us free to believe in what You can do. Take all these small things that are almost invisible to us and make of them Your kingdom. Take all these discounted people who are almost invisible to us and make of them Your family.

In Your grace, include us too—for we are very small.

Day 62

REMEMBERING

So Joshua summoned the twelve men he had selected from the Israelites, one man for each tribe, and said to them, "Go across to the ark of the LORD your God in the middle of the Jordan. Each of you lift a stone onto his shoulder, one for each of the Israelite tribes, so that this will be a sign among you. In the future, when your children ask you, 'What do these stones mean to you?' you should tell them, 'The waters of the Jordan were cut off in front of the ark of the LORD's covenant. When it crossed the Jordan, the Jordan's waters were cut off.' Therefore these stones will always be a memorial for the Israelites."

JOSHUA 4:4–7

It was an unforgettable moment: seven people gathered in secrecy in an abandoned, shelled-out building in the heart of Mogadishu for the purpose of sharing together the Lord's Supper. We were simply doing what Jesus' followers had done for almost two thousand years, sharing a simple meal to remember and celebrate Christ's willing and sacrificial death on the cross.

Followers of Jesus do this often. Followers of Jesus have done this repeatedly ever since Jesus gave His instructions to keep this act of memory alive.

But sharing the Lord's Supper in this setting at this time seemed almost impossible even to imagine.

We ate the bread in memory of Jesus' body, broken for us. We drank juice in remembrance of Jesus' blood, poured out for us. We talked quietly and simply about what Jesus had done for us—and we talked about what it meant to be His follower in a place like Somalia. We knew that our setting was quite different than what many followers of Jesus know—but we also knew that our setting was not unique today and throughout history. For centuries, believers in persecution have gathered secretly to share the Supper. We thought about those people as we gathered that day.

Jesus' instruction for us to remember is so very important. The Passover provides an opportunity for God's people to remember their rescue from Egypt. The stones that are described in Joshua 4 become a memorial to God's provision of His people as they enter the Land of Promise. And the Lord's Supper calls us to remembrance as we think about what Jesus has done so that we might experience forgiveness and abundant life.

We claim that we will never forget. Sadly, however we *do* forget. So God, in His grace, provides us with repeated meals and events and celebrations that help us remember.

We not only remember what Jesus did for us on the cross, but also how God has carried us over the years—how God has worked—how God has provided—how God has been faithful. Sharing the Supper in Mogadishu that day, we thought back on years of struggle and effort and strain, and we remembered and celebrated our faithful God.

Bread and juice. A pile of rocks. A special place. A favorite word of Scripture. A photograph. A song. A seashell. So many things can help us remember. And that is exactly what God wants us to do; He wants us to remember.

So we keep eating that bread. And we keep drinking from that cup.

Though we tend to be a forgetful people, God Himself will help us remember.

Lord God, we say that we will never forget. But that is simply not true. We do forget. We have forgotten. Help us to remember.

Only with great effort do we remember even important things. Yet, we dare not forget what You have done. Thank You for calling us. Thank You for providing us with living pictures that help us remember. When we see a rainbow, we think of Your promises. When we see a pile of rocks, we think of the impossible things that You have done. When we eat the bread, we remember Your grace. When we drink the cup, we are overwhelmed by Your love.

Lord God, fill our lives with memories of who You are and what You have done. Shout Your presence and power into our stopped-up ears . . . so that we might remember and never forget.

Day 63

DREAMS THAT OPEN DOORS

After these events, the word of the LORD
came to Abram in a vision . . .
GENESIS 15:1A

Bhandari was born in Nepal. He now lives in another country and is a devoted follower of Jesus. His family heritage includes priests from both the Hindu and Buddhist traditions. When we met Bhandari, we could not imagine how he had ever found Jesus–or, more the point, how Jesus had ever found him! At the first opportunity, we asked him to tell us his story.

Bhandari began his story by talking about his life long ago in Nepal. At that time, he had no access to Jesus at all. Family traditions guided his life and, like most people in his village, Bhandari simply followed the path that was laid out for him.

He explained, though, that when he was about fifteen years old, he began to have dreams. The dreams he had were troubling dreams, telling him plainly that things were not right in his life. His dreams led him to no specific next steps; they simply left him with a feeling of incompleteness and a desire for something more. At that time, he did not know what the dreams meant—nor what to do in response. What he did know, however, was that he needed something that he did not have.

Dreams are a common element in faith stories around the world. Sometimes, seekers will be given very specific instructions in a dream.

They might be told, for example, to find Jesus. They might be told to find the gospel. They might even be told to find a Bible. In Bhandari's case, however, there were no clear instructions; his dreams simply led him to search for something that would make him whole.

These dreams continued for several years. Even as he grew older and eventually moved from place to place, the unsettling dreams continued. (While he told his story very slowly and with great detail, we wondered when and where Jesus would show up!) Sure enough, when Bhandari was a young man, he met a foreign worker in another country. At the time, he thought the meeting was a simple coincidence. Looking back now, however, he knows that this meeting was arranged by God.

After years of looking for something that he could not even name or identify, Bhandari heard about Jesus from this worker. When he heard the story of Jesus, he knew immediately that his quest was finished. He knew that this was exactly what he had been searching for. At that very point, his dreams stopped. Never again did he have that dream that left him feeling empty, the dream that pushed him to search.

The witness of the worker was essential in Bhandari's coming to faith in Jesus. But interestingly, it was the repeated dream that caused him to search in the first place.

God has so many different ways of reaching people. God can reach people through a verbal witness, through the Bible, through the simple prompting of the Holy Spirit, through a miracle, or through an act of healing. And God can also use dreams to accomplish His purposes.

In the case of Bhandari, it was a repeated dream that set him on a mission to find Jesus.

*Lord God, since the earliest days You have used dreams to
communicate with people and draw them to Yourself. What
You have done, You still do. Thank You for finding a way
to lead people on the path that leads to friendship with
You. Thank You for Your creativity in reaching people.*

*As You pursue people and draw them forward, help us to find
our place in that holy process. Help us to be ready to speak when
You send someone to us. Teach us that divine appointments
are not coincidental. Lord Jesus, let us dream again.*

Day 64

OPPORTUNITY IN OPPOSITION

I will come to you after I pass through Macedonia—for I will be traveling through Macedonia—and perhaps I will remain with you or even spend the winter, so that you may send me on my way wherever I go. I don't want to see you now just in passing, since I hope to spend some time with you, if the Lord allows. But I will stay in Ephesus until Pentecost, because a wide door for effective ministry has opened for me—yet many oppose me.

1 CORINTHIANS 16:5–9

Many people presume that the most effective ministry happens when opposition is at a minimum. In the presence of opposition—especially significant opposition—we tend to walk away, and search for a place that seems more conducive to productive service.

Paul's words near the conclusion of 1 Corinthians, however, remind us of something we have heard often. In our interviews, many people spoke of situations where opposition was great, and rather than looking for a better situation, many of these brothers and sisters remained faithful, and, as a result, experienced wonderful fruit in ministry. This seems to be exactly what the apostle Paul is suggesting in the closing words of his letter.

As he comes to the end of 1 Corinthians, Paul reflects on his plans. He wanted to visit his friends in Corinth, but only if he had sufficient time for an extended visit. Since he didn't have the time for that, he decided to remain in Ephesus.

On the one hand, he saw that "a wide door for effective ministry" had opened for him. On the other hand, he was aware of significant opposition. How interesting that both of those realities can be present at the same time. And how amazing that both of those realities are, in fact, often present at the same time!

The potential for effective ministry . . . right in the middle of great opposition.

The presence of significant opposition does not cause Paul to leave. In fact, the presence of opposition does not even cause Paul to *want* to leave. Instead, he is compelled to stay—even in the presence of opposition—because he sees the potential for significant ministry.

While people might normally take the path of least resistance, persecuted followers of Jesus told us repeatedly that opposition and opportunity often appear close together. What's more, they explained that avoiding opposition wasn't always the best approach. In fact, sometimes stepping away from opposition would mean stepping away from ministry.

Evidently, walking away is not always the best approach. Sometimes, as followers of Jesus, we need to stay at our post even in the face of opposition.

Father, we trust You to guide us. We trust You to show us the way. When it is time to walk away from opposition, we pray that You would give us the wisdom to see—and the courage to leave. But when it is time to stay, we pray that You would enable us to do just that.

Give us insight as we try to understand that opposition is sure to come. Teach us that opposition is not always an indication that we have done something wrong. Help us to consider the possibility that opposition might, in fact, indicate that we are exactly where we should be.

Whether there is opposition or not, help us to be faithful.

Day 65

DESPERATE

*Listen, LORD, and answer me, for I am poor and
needy. Protect my life, for I am faithful. You are my
God; save your servant who trusts in you. Be gracious
to me, Lord, for I call to you all day long. Bring joy to
your servant's life, because I appeal to you, Lord.*

PSALM 86:1–4

Just a few weeks after sharing that secret Lord's Supper with the small group in Mogadishu, we learned that the four Somali believers who had gathered with us that day had been martyred. In what was clearly a coordinated assassination plot, all four attacks had been launched within minutes of each other on the same morning. A radical Muslim group claimed credit. To add further cruelty, the murderers had stolen the bodies of the men they had assassinated. Not one of the bodies was ever found.

Before this terrible event happened, we were already in the depths of discouragement. Suddenly, though, we felt what can only be called despair. Even our view of the world changed; all we could see was destruction, suffering, and hopelessness. We could find little grace in our hearts—and we struggled to understand how God could continue to remain gracious.

God met us in our heartache.

Our initial response was one of anger. We thought of those who had caused such senseless grief—and we felt like praying that they would experience harsh consequences for their sin. Even in our anger, though, God reminded us of *our own* sin—and God reminded us of how undeserving *we* were of His grace. He also reminded us that He is always able, and always at work—even in the depths of the most grievous pain and loss.

Many of the psalms express the kind of anguish that we were feeling. Psalm 86 is not quite as emotional as some of the other psalms, but it still expresses a sense of profound need. In these simple words, David is clear about his need—and he is just as clear about God's ability to intervene, act, rescue, and help. What David does best is to articulate those two great truths: our immense need and God's ability to make things different.

Interestingly, in this psalm, David does not tell God what to do. He does not tell God what would address his need. He does not advise God how to heal his hurt. Instead, David simply pleads for help. David is aware that his own perspective is limited, so he wisely decides to leave things in God's hands.

Declaring his need—and affirming God's ability to save—is all there is. And it is enough.

The heart and soul of David's need is simply this: "I am poor and needy." David is desperate for God's help. And he knows that God is his only hope.

That is exactly where we were: poor and needy, desperate for God's help, searching for some hint of hope in the darkness.

Merciful God, You are our only hope. We do not feel comfortable admitting that we are desperate—but desperate is what we are. We are poor. We are needy. Without Your help, we are lost. There is not much more to say. We could remind You that we are Your children. We could tell stories of what You have done in the past. We could even tell You what we think You should do.

But we choose not to do any of those things today.

Today, our prayer is simple and short. We are poor. We are needy. We are desperate for Your help. Help us to see things the way You see things. Merciful God, You are our only hope.

NOTHING SPECIAL

*"I am the Lord's servant," said Mary. "May it
be done to me according to your word."*

LUKE 1:38A

Because of the marvelous opportunities that we have had to talk with persecuted followers of Jesus all over the world, people sometimes see us as experts. While we have certainly learned a great deal in our travels and experiences, we continue to learn much more than we teach. Originally, we thought that we might be able to share wisdom with believers in persecution around the world, but we quickly came to understand that we were the learners, not the teachers.

And that is still true today. Even as we share what we have learned, we continue to stand before God with deep humility. Just in case you are wondering, our uniqueness is that we both have PhDs in what not to do. My wife loathes conflict, while I revel in what I call "recreational arguing." I have even suggested that it become an Olympic sport! Humility comes hard for me while Ruth exemplifies that particular fruit of the Spirit.

That admission, though, is a good reminder for all of us. We live in a world that values people who seem to know everything, people who claim to have all the answers. Our world sees honest and sincere humility as a weakness. In that, we are reminded once again that God's ways are not our ways.

Even so, God intends for His people to clothe themselves with humility—an attitude that is essential if God is going to have His way with us. By choice, God's people are gracious with opinions—and gracious even with convictions. We live that way not because we are unclear about the truth, but because we wouldn't presume to know fully the mind of God. By choice, we refuse to judge others—not because we are uncertain of what is right and wrong, but because we would not presume to put ourselves in God's place. By choice, we guard ourselves every day against the sin of pride—not because we have low self-esteem, but because we esteem God and God alone.

In Ephesians 3:8, the apostle Paul expressed this essential quality of humility in a single phrase. He called himself "the least of all the saints."

That attitude opens the door for ministry. That attitude opens the door for the sharing of our faith. That attitude makes community possible. That attitude reveals whether or not God is actually having His way with us.

As we consider the wonder of being brought into friendship with God, we should be able to say something like this: "Of all the people God might have chosen to love, I am the least deserving."

Humility may not get us very far in our world today. But without humility, our ministry will be severely weakened.

What a gift to know that we have been included—both in God's family and in the work that He places in our hands. Not because we deserve it or because we have earned it or because our inclusion is rightfully ours—but because of God's grace.

That realization is enough to make us different people. And that realization makes it possible for God to use us in His work.

We are, after all, the least of all the saints. But thanks be to God for His amazing grace—His grace that reaches even us!

*God of Grace, thank You for including us. Thank
You for making me part of Your family. Thank
You for inviting me to share in Your work.*

*Keep me from pride. Teach me that I do not deserve Your
grace. Remind me daily that I am nothing special—except
for the fact that You have called me to be Your own.*

Day 67

GOD HAS HIS REASONS

*"This is so that all the peoples of the earth may
know that the LORD's hand is mighty, and so that
you may always fear the LORD your God."*

JOSHUA 4:24

The question that kept us up many nights . . . *WHY?*

After meeting so many people, after hearing so many stories, after mourning unspeakable suffering and loss, after celebrating astounding victory, after being reminded over and over again of God's ability to accomplish His purposes—we struggled to grasp and understand God's unusual ways. Assured by Scripture that God's ways are, in fact, unusual, we wanted to understand why exactly God does what He does.

Even more, why would God use suffering to accomplish His purposes? And how could even persecution be a tool that God could use for His glory?

Again, it was the persecuted believers in China who helped us in our struggle. Their attitude toward persecution was quite surprising. Instead of fearing persecution or allowing persecution to prevent witness, believers in China simply saw persecution as the inevitable outcome of a faithful life. To be sure, these believers never sought persecution; they never went out of their way to cause trouble or attract attacks. All the same, they understood that faithful obedience to the call of Jesus would eventually lead to this result. It was their understanding that, for faithful followers of Jesus, persecution was *inevitable*. For them, the only possible way to avoid persecution was to deny their faith and to be silent about their relationship with Jesus.

Clearly, that was a choice they would not make.

They explained it to us this way:

> Once they start meeting as believers in a home, the security forces will threaten them. The authorities will say, "You must stop meeting! If you do not stop meeting, we will take away your home."
>
> In response, the believers will answer: "If you take away our home, we will be free to trust in Jesus because this home belongs to Him."
>
> That answer will confuse the security forces. They will then say, "We can't talk to this Jesus, but we can certainly make things hard for you. Without your home, your family will have nowhere to live."
>
> The believers will respond: "Then we will be free to trust Jesus for our shelter and for our daily bread."
>
> The authorities will then respond: "If you keep this up, we will beat you."
>
> The response of the believers—at this point predictable—"Then we will be free to trust Jesus for our healing."
>
> "Then we will put you in prison!"
>
> "Then we will be free to trust Jesus while we are in prison. In fact, we will plant churches in prison!"
>
> "Then we will kill you!"
>
> "Then we will be free to go to Jesus in heaven and be with Him forever."

The believers were not trying to be cute or clever. They were not making light of their suffering or potential suffering. They were simply bearing witness to the way that God works in the lives of His people. They were acknowledging that true freedom is never the purview of a government. The source of true freedom is the throne of God.

The river rocks mentioned in Joshua 4 were an enduring symbol and sign for God's people. Those rocks established a perpetual memory of the crossing of the Jordan River—and that crossing is explicitly linked to the crossing of the Red Sea that had happened earlier. These parallel events highlight the ability of God to take care of His people, and accomplish His purposes. The river rocks were intended to guarantee that God's people would always remember what God had done.

Behind that affirmation, however, is our question: *Why? Why does God do what He does?*

According to Joshua 4:24, there are two answers to that question:

> First, God does what He does *so that all the people of the earth may know that the Lord's hand is mighty.* We already know that, of course. But the peoples of the earth do not know that. So, first, God does what He does so that the whole world might know of His power.

> Second, God does what He does *so that we may always fear the Lord our God.* To fear means to hold in the highest reverence, to stand before God in awe, to live before Him with obedience and worship.

So why does God do what He does? Why does God go to such lengths to reach this broken world? Why does God allow His children to suffer, and why does He use that suffering for His purposes? Why has God determined to use even persecution for His purposes?

There may be many answers, but these two answers are a great starting point.

> God does what He does *so that all the people of the earth may know that the Lord's hand is mighty.*

> And God does what He does *so that we may always fear the Lord our God.*

Lord God, we are undone in Your presence. To imagine that the Creator of all things desires a friendship with us is beyond our comprehension. All we can do is bow before You—overwhelmed by Your grace. In the same moment, it dawns on us that we have the high privilege of helping others experience this same grace.

Help us not to be selfish with Your priceless gift. Help us to embrace any sacrifice that You put before us. Empower us to share and go and give and tell, so that others might know of Your power.

We pray that our lives today might be an honest and true expression of our love for You. May everything we do and everything we say be an act of worship—because You are worthy. You alone are worthy.

Day 68

PASSING ON YOUR STORY

"These words that I am giving you today are to be in your heart. Repeat them to your children. Talk about them when you sit in your house and when you walk along the road, when you lie down and when you get up."

DEUTERONOMY 6:6–7

When seventy-year-old Katya began to tell us the story of her life with Jesus, we stopped her immediately and encouraged her to gather her children and her grandchildren so that they might hear her story at the same time. It turned out that her family had never heard the narrative related to her family's faith. It was important that they know about the faithfulness of their mother and grandmother.

Once the family had gathered, Katya related generations of faith-filled lives to those listening intently to her story.

She told the account of her grandfather's arrest in 1917 by officials of the USSR. Katya was seven years old at the time. Her grandfather was warned by a friend within the security police that he would be arrested for being a pastor. He used that final day of freedom to get his affairs in order, and to bury the family Bible in the field behind the house. He couldn't bear the thought of that treasure being taken by the authorities.

Several weeks later, Katya's family was given permission to see him in prison. As he said good-bye to his family, he secretly slipped a note to his wife, through the chain link fence, that revealed where he had hidden the family's Bible. The note told Katya's grandmother to dig up the Bible, to gather the whole family together, and to read the pages that had been hidden inside the Bible's front cover. After the family returned home, they dug up the buried Bible. Together, they read the testimony that her grandfather had placed in the Bible, as well as his strong encouragement to remain faithful to God no matter what.

As they read the words written in that Bible, the family could not have imagined that this pastor, husband, father, and grandfather would be put to death inside the prison in just two weeks. The visit they shared with him that day was the last time any of them saw him alive.

Even though that had happened more than seventy years earlier, Katya still remembered it well. And she told his story of faith to her own extended family. They sat in amazement as they heard their family's story of faith and obedience even in the face of great suffering and sacrifice.

The last words her grandfather had written on his note in the Bible came from Revelation 2:10, "Be faithful unto death" (RSV).

Hearing the story, her daughter told Katya how proud she was. Katya's grandchildren gathered around her and hugged her. They admired, appreciated, and honored the courage and bravery of their grandmother, of their entire family, and of their great-great-grandfather.

The story that had essentially defined Katya's entire life was now being passed on to her children and her grandchildren. They already knew bits and pieces of her background, of course. But they had never heard before the whole story of her life.

Hearing that story helped them grow in their faith and understand more deeply the ways of God. What a gift it was to watch a genealogy of faith being passed down to the next generation in that two-room apartment as Katya told her family's testimony of faith and sacrifice.

Lord God, You are not only the God of history—You are also the God of our personal history. Your activity in our lives is the heart of our story. Help us to be bold and winsome in the telling of our story.

Sometimes it seems easier to tell our story to people we don't know very well. But we understand that the people who are close to us need to hear our story as well. Help us to not keep our story to ourselves. Allow us to build a genealogy of faith for our family and friends.

Thank You for what You have done in our lives. Thank You for what You continue to do. Set us free to talk about it—especially with those who are closest to us. Lord, may we be "faithful unto death."

Day 69

ABIDING

"I am the vine; you are the branches. The one who
remains in me and I in him produces much fruit,
because you can do nothing without me."

JOHN 15:5

How does a severely persecuted follower of Jesus keep the faith? How does a person endure physical and psychological torture? How does a person survive separation from family members and even imprisonment? How does a believer handle intense isolation and loneliness? How does a person come to a point where it might be possible to pray for the persecutors and love them with the love of Jesus?

How is that possible?

How can you share your faith in a world where people are not always eager to hear a word about Jesus? How can you risk your time and money for the cause of Christ? How can you put yourself in situations that might be risky or costly or even dangerous? How would it be possible for you to consider leaving your home to travel far away in obedience to the call of Jesus? How would it be possible for you to embrace a life of sacrifice and suffering—when you could easily choose a life of comfort and ease instead?

How is that possible?

There is only one answer to those questions. That kind of life is possible only if we remain in Jesus and He remains in us (John 15:5).

Jesus invites His children into a life of intimate relationship. As we journey, we journey with Jesus. As we journey, we walk in step with Him. He never leaves us. Instead, He promises to be with us every moment.

Forever.

Even in our desire to be obedient to Jesus' call, it is possible for us to become consumed with other matters. After all, there are details to manage, strategies to develop, programs to plan, approaches to ministry to consider, commitments to honor. In addition, there are the overwhelming tasks of life itself.

And all of that is important.

But it all pales in comparison to the most important thing: our personal, intimate relationship with Jesus. There is no way to fulfill our calling—there is no way to be obedient—there is no way to live a life of God-honoring sacrifice . . . unless we abide in Jesus.

Year by year. Month by month. Week by week. Day by day. Moment by moment.

As we abide in Jesus, He shapes us. As we abide in Jesus, He changes us. As we abide in Jesus, He uses us. As we abide in Jesus, He redefines who we are and what we value. As we abide in Jesus, we become the people He created us to be.

And that all starts with the simple choice. It won't happen by accident—or even by habit. It is something that we must choose each day.

Lord Jesus, we long to stay close to You. We choose to abide in You. We desire to walk in step with You.

We understand that we have a high calling. We understand that it is crucial that we obey. We understand that we simply must be obedient and faithful. But we also understand that a life like that is impossible unless we abide in You.

Give us wisdom so that we might know that abiding in You is our first and only priority. Allow "being in Christ" to define us.

Day 70

Praying inside the Fish

*"I called to the LORD in my distress, and he answered me. I
cried for help from deep inside Sheol; you heard my voice."
"I sank to the foundations of the mountains, the
earth's gates shut behind me forever! Then you
raised my life from the Pit, LORD my God!"
"But as for me, I will sacrifice to you with a
voice of thanksgiving. I will fulfill what I have
vowed. Salvation belongs to the LORD."*

Jonah 2:2, 6, 9

✝ One of the key parts of our interviews with persecuted
followers of Jesus focused on their reactions and responses
in times of despair. We were eager to hear about their choices, their
attitudes, and their behaviors when hope was hard to find. How did
these faithful brothers and sisters move forward? How did they survive?
What kept them going?

As we listened, the story of Jonah came to mind. In Jonah's case,
his suffering was caused by his own disobedience. Sent by God to
Nineveh, Jonah came up with his own plan and sought passage on a
ship headed for Tarshish. After a great storm, Jonah was thrown into
the sea—and we're told that God "appointed a great fish to swallow
Jonah, and Jonah was in the belly of the fish three days and three
nights" (Jonah 1:17).

During those three days and three nights—inside the fish—Jonah prayed. Jonah was eventually rescued—and we can read about that rescue in Jonah 2:10.

But so much of Jonah's prayer—even though his rescue hadn't happened yet—was prayed as if the rescue had already happened!

We are wise to pay attention to the verb tenses in Jonah's prayer. *The Lord answered me. The Lord heard my voice. The Lord raised my life from the Pit.* These things had not yet happened when Jonah prayed these words—and yet Jonah prayed these words as if God's rescue had already happened.

We sensed that same attitude with many of the persecuted followers of Jesus that we talked with. They were willing to praise God *even before they had experienced God's rescue*! Somehow, they had learned to pray prayers of thanksgiving in the past tense—fully trusting that God's promises were sure and certain . . . even before those promises came to pass.

It is one thing to praise God after the storm is over. But it is another thing altogether to praise God while the storm is still raging. Persecuted brothers and sisters in Christ—and Jonah—teach us the wisdom of praying prayers of thanksgiving even as the storm continues, even while we wait for God's rescue.

Sometimes it feels like we are thrashing around in the sea—like we are inside the fish. Our setting, however, really doesn't matter. We are invited to pray as if God's rescue has already happened.

Salvation comes from the Lord. That's easy to see after the rescue has taken place. But God's people know that to be true even when we are waiting for Him to show up.

Promise-making and Promise-keeping God, thank You for teaching us that Your Word stands true forever. Teach us to cling to You no matter what is happening around us. Teach us to pray prayers of thanksgiving in the past tense—certain that You will do everything You say.

Transform my halting unbelief into strong and steady trust. In our despair, give us hope.

Day 71

Praying for the Persecutors: Step One

*But I trust in you, LORD; I say, "You are my God." The
course of my life is in your power; rescue me from the power
of my enemies and from my persecutors. Make your face
shine on your servant; save me by your faithful love.*

Psalm 31:14–16

We were intrigued when persecuted followers of Jesus
began to talk about their persecutors. What was especially
interesting was how these persecuted believers reacted to their persecution, how they treated those who caused them such pain, and how they
prayed. In most cases, their prayers were far beyond what we could
imagine was even possible. We have learned much about the kingdom
of God by listening to believers in persecution pray. At the same time,
we began to identify at least five specific kinds of prayers that were
mentioned.

All five of these prayers are represented in Scripture. Some are pre-
sented as examples of greater maturity and godliness. It was instructive
to note the progression that we heard in our interviews.

In most cases, the initial prayer in situations of persecution was a
simple prayer requesting rescue by God. When we are threatened and
under attack, it is only natural to think of personal survival—and it is
only natural to reach out to God and ask for deliverance, rescue, and
salvation.

That is precisely what the psalmist does in Psalm 31:14–16. In situations of suffering, this kind of praying makes perfect sense. We know that God loves us. We know that God is aware of our situation. We know that God knows all about the people who are causing us harm. And in light of all that we know, we reach out to God and ask for help. Clearly, this is often the first prayer that we pray—but we will typically pray this prayer only after we have expended our resources and done everything that we can do to overcome the challenge that we face. Often our first response to persecution is to turn to help from governments, and the forces they command, to rescue us and other believers from the persecutors. While Jesus prayed for the "cup to pass," it is important to note that His response to the coming persecution was one of prayer to His Father.

For persecuted believers, this was also the first prayer: a simple request for God's salvation. "God, save us!" These words came from Scripture and these words revealed the most basic need of those who were suffering because of their faith.

Lord God, save us! No words could come to our lips more naturally or more easily. We have known Your salvation and Your rescue and Your deliverance. We are certain that You know the pain that Your children bear.

In persecution and in other seasons of heartache, we ask for Your help. And we trust You to respond because You are gracious and because we are Your beloved children.

Lord God, save us!

PRAYING FOR THE PERSECUTORS: STEP TWO

*LORD, do not let me be disgraced when I call on
you. Let the wicked be disgraced; let them be quiet
in Sheol. Let lying lips that arrogantly speak against
the righteous in proud contempt be silenced.*

PSALM 31:17–18

In the previous devotional, we found the psalmist praying for God's rescue. As his prayer continues, we now find the psalmist asking that God judge and punish those who wage war against the righteous. The psalmist calls those people "wicked," and he longs to see them disgraced. He wants to see them get what they deserve.

We heard this prayer also in our interviews. They knew how highly God values justice, and their prayers reflected both the conviction that God knew exactly what was happening and that God was able to make things right. Part of making things right, they believed, was God's judgment of the persecutors. This prayer is a far cry from another prayer that we would also hear in the interviews ("Father, forgive them!")—but this is a prayer that is surely understandable, justified, and completely in line with what we encounter in Scripture.

Especially when we are experiencing righteous suffering, it is appropriate and fitting to ask God for justice. Of course, while God would love to see us rise above this kind of prayer—it is also fair to believe that God would understand why our prayers would include words like these.

"God, save me" and "God, punish the evil ones" are understandable requests from believers in persecution. Yes, these are also the prayers we, the church, and those reporting on persecution offer on behalf of our persecuted family. Rescue and punishment often describe the Western church's response to the persecution of others. The challenge is that we get stuck in a mode of rescue and punishment rather than learning from our brothers and sisters in persecution. We pity their plight and we want to rescue them to a safe Western environment, leaving the wolves void of witness by the sheep Jesus has placed in their midst.

We learned that believers in persecution certainly prayed for justice; they sincerely hoped that God would judge the persecutors. However, we never heard examples of persecuted believers taking justice into their own hands. Even as they prayed these words, they were satisfied leaving ultimate outcomes in God's hands. They seemed content to pray that their persecutors would be judged; having prayed that prayer, they left their desire with God and trusted Him to do what was best.

In almost every case, this was not the final prayer related to the persecutors. There were more prayers on the horizon. Believers in persecution do not become stuck in the deliverance and punishment battle between good and evil.

Surely, this makes good sense to us. When others do us harm—however that happens—it is fitting to take our pain to God and ask that He determine what is right and what is wrong.

As we grow in our faith, we strive to pray deeper prayers, of course. But praying for justice in seasons of suffering is entirely understandable.

God, we know that there are deeper prayers to pray—but we also know that it is right and good to bring our pain to You. We often presume to know how You should deal with those who cause destruction and suffering—and sometimes our prayers are raw and ragged. We also know that we are often deserving of Your judgment. Still, we ask that You take notice of those who cause damage to Your children.

Even as we pray these kinds of prayers, call us to something deeper, richer, higher. Draw our attention to the heart and attitude of Jesus—and teach us to pray like Him.

Day 73

PRAYING FOR THE PERSECUTORS: STEP THREE

Then Jesus said, "Father, forgive them, because they do not know what they are doing."

LUKE 23:34A

✝ Yet another prayer that we heard in the interviews echoed the words of Jesus on the cross. Clearly, something significant had happened in the hearts of these believers in persecution that empowered them to pray this third very different prayer. There was never an effort to diminish or downplay the extent of the suffering or the evil behavior of the persecutors, but a spiritual shift had taken place. Prayers for personal rescue and prayers for justice moved into the background—and their hearts' desire was for forgiveness. Their prayers reflected a growing intimacy with Jesus and His example in similar situations.

Completely in line with Jesus' teaching in the Sermon on the Mount, the suffering believer begins to pray not *against* the persecutors, but *for* them. And the specific request is that they would be forgiven. Again, this prayer echoes the very words of Jesus on the cross.

In an earlier devotional, we told the story of four dear friends, all Somali believers, who were murdered on the same day. These killings were deliberate and planned. Within one hour, all four of these friends were brutally put to death. Their murderers hid their bodies in order to deny them proper burials.

Crushed by the horror of this unspeakable evil, we cried out to God for justice. We were broken and angry. Even though we knew that God was fully aware of what had happened, we poured out the details to Him. In our brokenness, we concluded that, in light of what had happened, no one in all Somalia was worthy of God's grace.

In that moment, God spoke clearly to us: "You are not worthy of My grace either!"

We had a hard time comparing our sin with the sin that we had just observed in those killings, but God did a work in our hearts. He reminded us of the undeserved forgiveness that we had experienced—and He called us to pray prayers of forgiveness for those who had done such evil. Honestly, this was very hard to do. The prayers that we felt led to pray were very hard. It was not part of our natural inclination to intercede for persecutors.

But we were compelled to follow the example of Jesus.

We prayed to God and we begged Him for strength.

And then we prayed that God would forgive those who had destroyed the lives of our four dear friends. Such an impossible prayer flowed from Jesus' command to "love our enemies."

Forgiving God, remind us that we do not deserve Your grace. Remind us of our sin. Remind us of the love that You have revealed through the cross of Jesus.

Aware of our own sin, give us the courage to love and ask for forgiveness for others. It will take great courage to pray this way—because it is very hard for us. Even so, we want our prayers to sound like Jesus' prayer on the cross.

Help us to pray that way.

Day 74

PRAYING FOR THE PERSECUTORS: STEP FOUR

"And forgive us our debts, as we also have forgiven our debtors."
"For if you forgive others their offenses, your heavenly
Father will forgive you as well. But if you don't forgive
others, your Father will not forgive your offenses."

MATTHEW 6:12, 14–15

Another uncommon prayer that surfaced in our interviews called to mind Jesus' words about prayer in the Sermon on the Mount. It was as if believers in persecution were intentionally attempting to model exactly what Jesus taught. Clearly, this was humanly impossible. But believers in persecution explained that they were being empowered by the Spirit of God to do what was humanly impossible.

Not only were these persecuted followers of Jesus praying for forgiveness for their persecutors, they were also coming to understand that there was a connection between their forgiveness of others and God's forgiveness of them.

When we come to a profound and personal awareness of our own sin—when we come to understand the cost of God's forgiveness in our own lives—then we are ready to extend His forgiveness to others . . . even to others who have done us great harm.

In truth, this is a frightening thing to pray: that we want God to forgive us *in the same way* that we have forgiven others! For most of us, that would not be a wise thing to pray. We know that our forgiveness of others is often half-hearted, insincere, begrudgingly given, incomplete. And we would never want God's forgiveness of our sin to be like that. So it makes sense that we would hesitate before praying for the kind of forgiveness that we have given to others. Still, this is exactly what we are told to pray. And praying these words compels us to extend a forgiveness to others that is rich and full and free . . . and painfully difficult.

Amazingly, we met believers in persecution who were willing to pray exactly that way. Amazingly, we met believers in persecution who had learned to extend to their oppressors a forgiveness that was rich and full and free. Evidently, God had done such a work in their hearts that they were able to say these words joyfully and without hesitation: "Lord God, forgive us *in the same way* that we have forgiven our persecutors."

Other than the power of God, there is no way to pray this prayer.

God, we tend to see our sin as small and insignificant. And we tend to see the sins of others as large and weighty. As a result, we imagine that we deserve Your forgiveness—and that others don't. And when we see things that way, it makes perfect sense for us to withhold our forgiveness of others . . . because they do not really deserve it.

Your words are clear—but we have such a hard time believing that there is a connection between our forgiveness of others and Your forgiveness of us. Having experienced Your gracious forgiveness, though, we cannot help but extend that same forgiveness to others.

No one deserves Your forgiveness. We do not deserve Your forgiveness. Persecutors do not deserve Your forgiveness. But You are full of grace and mercy.

Day 75

PRAYING FOR THE PERSECUTORS: STEP FIVE

"Now my soul is troubled. What should I say—
Father, save me from this hour? But that is why I
came to this hour. Father, glorify your name."

JOHN 12:27–28A

As we listened carefully to the prayers of the persecuted, we eventually heard that many had come to a place where they would pray simply that God's name would be glorified.

Even in the depths of despair—and facing severe physical and psychological suffering—these believers were focused on God's glory. This attitude is reflected in the words of the Lord's Prayer when Jesus invites us to "honor the Father's name as holy" (see Matt. 6:9).

This kind of prayer embraces what Jesus has said about suffering for the faith: both that such suffering is sure to come, and that God will use even persecution for His purposes. What becomes most important is not the personal circumstance of suffering or even God's judgment of the persecutor, but the ultimate outcome that is made possible and assured by God. Somehow—no matter what happens—God will use even persecution to further His kingdom and fulfill His plans.

Especially in the face of persecution, this is a radical—though completely biblical—prayer. Knowing how the Father could use even the grievous pain of Jesus' cross for ultimate good, we can understand how God can use even persecution for His purposes. We heard from many suffering believers who had been so drawn into this mystery that they were willing to pray that God would somehow be glorified even in and through their persecution.

This prayer also teaches us that it is the believer's responsibility—and privilege—to glorify God regardless of the setting or environment. Sometimes, we feel that we can glorify God only when the circumstances are right or, perhaps, only when we are experiencing seasons of safety and political freedom. But persecuted believers have taught us that we can choose to bring glory to God regardless of our setting. Somehow, the persecuted believers that we talked with were determined to glorify God, even in settings of severe persecution.

While we would never want to seek persecution, we can be certain that God can use it for His purposes when it comes.

We would be wise to remember that persecution is the *inevitable* result of faithful obedience to Jesus. He has told us plainly that it will happen. But when it happens, we can be sure that God will use it to bring glory to His name.

Even more, we can pray for that very thing.

Father, we long to grow in our understanding of prayer. Teach us that our prayers can reflect not only our natural inclinations (for things like rescue and justice)—but that our prayers can also reflect Your purposes and plans. Set us free to love and pray for forgiveness—and especially to pray for Your glory.

You amaze us with Your ability to use the most unusual things for Your purposes. In Your hands, a cross becomes the carrier of grace. In Your hands, suffering can change people and change the world. In Your hands, persecution can be used to bring glory to Your name.

Thank You for reminding us of what You can do.

LEAVING ROOM FOR JOY

*"But for you who fear my name, the sun of righteousness
will rise with healing in its wings, and you will go out
and playfully jump like calves from the stall."*

MALACHI 4:2

Stoyan was about sixty years old when he told us his story.
Stoyan was a respected and well-known leader in his own
right, but much of his story was focused on his father. Clearly, the
faithfulness of Stoyan's father in the face of persecution had affected
him deeply. From his father, Stoyan had learned how to thrive as a
follower of Jesus despite intense and relentless opposition.

Stoyan's father had been arrested when the communists began con-
solidating their power throughout his country. Stoyan was twelve years
old when the authorities came for his father. His father's guards were
merciless in their mistreatment of him—mistreatment that left lasting
emotional, psychological, and physical scars. Somehow, Stoyan's father
remained strong. He refused to deny his faith. His strength carried
over to other members of his family. Stoyan's mother was resolute and
unshakable during those years of suffering. And Stoyan himself learned
to model his parents' commitment.

Eventually, Stoyan and his mother were evicted from their home and
forced to relocate to a distant village. Everything they owned was taken
away from them. But somehow their needs were met by God's gracious
care—care that often came through the generous help of other believers.

Stoyan had every right to be angry and bitter about the misery that had been inflicted upon his family. Much to our surprise, Stoyan's stories were thoroughly joyful and hopeful. He was deeply honest about the suffering that had followed him for decades, but somehow he refused to allow that suffering to define his life.

His life was defined not by all that pain, but by his love for Jesus.

Malachi 4 begins with images of judgment, failure, and sin. But those images quickly give way to a very different picture: a picture of joy and hope and promise. Malachi holds before the people the possibility of healing. He even talks about calves playfully jumping when released from the stall. What a captivating picture of life, vitality, freedom, and hopefulness! What a beautiful picture of joy!

Somehow, Stoyan was able to acknowledge the pain and suffering—and then shift his focus to the presence and power of God.

Somehow, Stoyan was able to choose joy.

God of Joy, forgive us for focusing so much on things that are hard. Even as we struggle, give us a glimpse of the life You offer us. Teach us the way of hope and freedom, the way of vitality and joy. Draw us close so that we might be like You.

Even if we do not literally playfully jump like a calf, help us to be a person of great joy. Remind us that our joyful hearts may actually bring joy to others. Help us to be careful about the way we live.

Even in this broken world—especially in this broken world—we rejoice in You!

Day 77

LATER

*Then Hezekiah turned his face to the wall and prayed to
the LORD. He said, "Please, LORD, remember how I have
walked before you faithfully and wholeheartedly, and
have done what pleases you." And Hezekiah wept bitterly.
Then the word of the LORD came to Isaiah: "Go and tell
Hezekiah that this is what the LORD God of your ancestor
David says: I have heard your prayer; I have seen your
tears. Look, I am going to add fifteen years to your life."*

ISAIAH 38:2–5

After several days of private interviews with persecuted house
church leaders in China, it dawned on us that something
especially holy was happening. Instead of continuing to do the
interviews in private, the leaders decided to gather an entire group
together and share their interview in a large group setting. We were
learning so much, and they wanted the others to hear what we were
hearing.

One theme that surfaced repeatedly in these interviews focused on
the urgency of sharing Jesus. According to the interviews, even when
these believers had been imprisoned for their faith, they saw sharing Jesus as their highest priority. And when they were released from
prison, it continued to be their highest priority. If they were suffering
economic hardship—or if they happened to be experiencing a season
of relative abundance—the priority never changed.

It was as if they had determined that they would share Jesus *no matter what*. And that commitment guided them through life.

Often, we struggle to find that kind of clarity in our own lives. We fail to live with that same sense of urgency. Even if we determine that sharing Jesus is important to us, we decide that we will do that *later . . . at some point in the future . . . one day.*

Or perhaps we will share Jesus *when our circumstances change.*

The Bible story that we read in Isaiah 38 is often celebrated as an illustration of answered prayer. And it is that! Hezekiah asks God for a delay in his impending death. And God, miraculously, answers Hezekiah's prayer. God grants Hezekiah an additional fifteen years of life.

And even as we praise God for the gift of answered prayer, we might also pause to wonder about how exactly Hezekiah would use those extra years. The Bible does not provide us with too much detail, so perhaps we are free to speculate.

Imagine those first few weeks after Hezekiah's answered prayer. He probably promised God that he would use his extra years well. People who endure a crisis often talk about "a second chance" or "a new lease on life." And that is likely where Hezekiah started.

Then, perhaps, the gift of his extra years grew a little dim as time passed. It probably became easy to forget the original crisis—and maybe it became easy even to forget the gift that God had granted. Fifteen years is a long time. New crises would have come up. Life would have gone on. And Hezekiah probably lost some of his earlier resolve.

Eventually, Hezekiah probably wondered if God would really hold to His plan and keep His "fifteen-year pronouncement." Like most people, Hezekiah probably began again to live as if he would live forever—believing that he would have time for the important things *later*.

While the Bible doesn't tell us everything that happened in Hezekiah's life, the next chapter of Isaiah paints a picture of a rather self-centered Hezekiah. Sadly, he was not deeply changed by the incredible miracle that happened in his life.

You and I have had an incredible miracle happen in our lives. The miracle is that we have heard about Jesus. We have experienced His grace. We have become His followers. We have made a commitment to tell others about Him.

And just like Hezekiah, we have a decision to make about how that miracle will affect the rest of our lives.

Sadly, we can forget it—and allow that miracle to fade into the background. We can assume that we have plenty of time to do all those important things that we know to do.

Or we can allow that miracle of God's activity in our lives to shape every moment of every day.

The persecuted believers in China taught us the value of this year, this day, this hour, this moment. For them, somehow, the miracle of God's grace never lost its luster. They never seemed to take it for granted. And sharing that miracle with others became their highest priority.

No matter what was happening in their lives, that remained their highest priority.

*Lord, we know better—but we live as if we
will live here on this earth forever.*

*There are so many things that we will get to . . . one day. There
are so many changes that we will make . . . one day. In fact, we
plan to get much more serious about obeying Your call . . . one
day. We plan to be bolder in our witness . . . one day. We plan
to make the Great Commission our commission . . . one day.*

But not today.

*I will do those important things later. Other
important things are my concern right now.*

*Once again, forgive us, Lord. Forgive us for the sin of
presumption—forgive us for assuming that we will have
plenty of time later. Forgive us for filling our lives with lesser
things. Forgive us for not seeing the urgency of this day.*

*Lord, what would you have us do today? Lord, how would you
have us live today? Lord, help us not waste this moment.*

Day 78

VISION

"Look at the nations and observe—be utterly
astounded! For I am doing something in your days
that you will not believe when you hear about it."

HABAKKUK 1:5

We often ask God to work. We often pray for God to intervene in situations that we're dealing with in our lives. We often ask that God would work around the world and make His name known. We often pray for a movement of God's Spirit—both in our lives and the lives of others.

Even as we ask for those good things, we can be frustrated by our inability to see the activity of God. But, as this devotional book reminds us, the problem isn't really God's inactivity—clearly, God is very much at work in His world!

Instead, the problem is our vision.

God is at work today in dramatic and startling ways. The story of His activity in the lives of believers in persecution around the world sounds very much like what we read in the Bible. Despite God's dramatic activity, though, our vision often lets us down. We have a hard time seeing. We have a hard time noticing. Sometimes we have a hard time paying attention. And often we simply cannot see what God is doing—even when something is happening right before our eyes.

One day, Jesus prayed out loud—and His prayer was followed by a voice from heaven! Other people heard the voice. Some people recognized that voice as a word from heaven. They heard it for what it was. But other people—people who had heard the very same thing—dismissed it. They said that the sound was simply thunder (John 12:27–29).

Sadly, that is what we often do. We watch God work; we actually see something that only God could do; we might even see a miracle. But then we find some way to dismiss the activity of God—or we discount what we have seen. All the while we continue to pray that God would work.

Through the prophet Habakkuk, God challenged the people to look around and pay attention. Whether they noticed it or not, God was on the move. He was doing something—and He was about to do something even more dramatic.

If we read a little further in Habakkuk, we discover that God was about to use the dreaded Chaldeans to accomplish His purpose. That would have been quite a surprise to learn that God would use people like the Chaldeans, but that simply serves as additional evidence that God is at work all around us. We shouldn't be surprised that God can use the Chaldeans for His purposes; after all, this is the same God who can use even persecution for His purposes!

We say that we want God to work. And there is nothing wrong with that request. But even while we pray that prayer, we need to pay attention to what God is already doing.

God essentially says, "Look around! Pay attention! Open your eyes! Notice all that I am doing. Be astonished! Be astounded! I am doing things that you will have a hard time believing! I am active right now. I am working right now. Open your eyes and see!"

*Lord God, give us vision. Help us to see what You
are doing. Help us to join You in Your work. Help
us to notice and pay attention and focus.*

*We confess that sometimes it seems that You are very quiet and that
You are not at work. But we know better. We know that You are
on the move. We know that You are doing what You have always
done. Give us eyes to see. Give us a heart that can respond.*

Give us vision.

Day 79

NO VOLUNTEERS

But you are a chosen race, a royal priesthood, a holy nation, a people for his possession, so that you may proclaim the praises of the one who called you out of darkness into his marvelous light.

1 PETER 2:9

Sometimes we make the mistake of thinking that we are being asked to volunteer for a task or assignment. We make the mistake of thinking that following Jesus is a matter of raising our hand.

But we are not volunteers at all. Followers of Jesus are the called, the chosen.

There are no volunteers among those who follow Jesus.

Oswald Chambers put it this way:

> Never choose to be a worker; but when God has put His call on you, woe be to you if you turn to the right hand or to the left. We are not here to work for God because we have chosen to do so, but because God has apprehended us.[4]

Perhaps it's hard to see the difference between volunteering and being called. If so, consider a few distinctions:

- A volunteer looks upon service as just one more thing to do, one more obligation to fulfill. The called are eager and ready to be used by God.

- A volunteer is offended by correction. The called are hungry to learn and grow—and will listen to godly counsel.

- A volunteer puts in minimum effort. The called give all they have.

- A volunteer complains when things are hard. The called embrace sacrifice in view of a higher goal.

- A volunteer is intimidated by the gifts of others. The called are secure in their calling and celebrate the variety of gifts that God can use.

- A volunteer is easily discouraged. In adversity, a volunteer might consider walking away. The called persevere.

- A volunteer might avoid situations that would require change. The called are always ready to be transformed.

There are many places to volunteer. There are many causes that we have the opportunity to embrace. There are many situations that provide us with a chance to serve. But the call of Jesus is something quite different. He chooses us. He enlists us. He gives us our assignment.

It is a wonderful thing to be invited to follow Jesus. But let us understand that answering His invitation is never a matter of volunteering.

After all, we are the called. There are no volunteers among those who follow Jesus.

Almighty God, You have chosen us. You have chosen us to receive life and grace and forgiveness. You have chosen us to be Your precious possession. And You have also chosen us for a high and holy task: to proclaim the praises of the One who has called us out of darkness into His marvelous light.

We embrace Your call. We celebrate Your call. We delight in Your call. And we obey Your call. We acknowledge Your right to use us as You please, to send us where You desire, and to shape us into the people You would have us be. We are not volunteers. We are called.

We pray that Your call on our lives would define everything we are and everything we do.

Day 80

OUR PLANS—OR HIS?

And they said to Jeremiah, "May the LORD be a true and faithful witness against us if we don't act according to every word the LORD your God sends you to tell us. Whether it is pleasant or unpleasant, we will obey the LORD our God to whom we are sending you so that it may go well with us. We will certainly obey the LORD our God!"

JEREMIAH 42:5–6

With research and the counsel of our Persecution Task Force, we gathered a list of forty-five countries that we hoped to visit. These were the countries where we expected to find significant oppression of believers. Obviously, this kind of extensive travel would require great planning—and we did our best to put together a workable and productive itinerary.

While our planning proved to be essential and helpful, we watched with amazement as God repeatedly reshaped all that we had planned. Sometimes interviews did not happen because believers had been recently arrested or had become ill. At other times, new people surfaced that we did not expect to meet. Sometimes borders between countries could not be crossed. Occasionally, even at the last minute, we went into a country that wasn't even on our original list.

Our planning was important, but God was guiding every step of our process. He had a remarkable way of making sure that we were in exactly the right place at the exactly the right time with exactly the right people.

Even while we were experiencing divine guidance in our own travels, we found ourselves talking with persecuted believers in many countries who had stories of their own about divine guidance in their lives. In one case, a Muslim Background Believer somehow learned that we had come to his country to talk with Muslims who had come to faith in Jesus. To this day, we have no idea how he possibly could have known that we were there. Even more, we have no idea how he could have found us. Somehow, though, through God's grace he did!

Against impossible odds, this man traveled for twenty-nine hours to tell us his story. And it revealed even more supernatural guidance from God. Years earlier, moved by a dream, he had been instructed to go to a faraway city. In the dream, he was told exactly where he would find someone who could tell him about Jesus. In his country, there were only a handful of believers from a people group of approximately twenty-one million. But the very specific instructions revealed in his dream led him to the exact location where one of those believers could be found. In that home, this Muslim man heard about Jesus—and he gave Jesus his life.

Our plans are important—but our plans are not nearly as important as the guidance of God.

And once we receive guidance from God, it is essential that we follow it.

In Jeremiah 42, we find the leaders of the people asking the prophet Jeremiah for guidance from God. Jerusalem had fallen, and the leaders wanted to know what they should do next. Their request (v. 3) of Jeremiah seems genuine. They assured Jeremiah that they would do whatever God told them to do (vv. 5–6).

We generally are quite eager to receive guidance from God—but we are especially happy when God's guidance lines up with whatever it is that we have already planned! Responding to the request of the leaders, Jeremiah gives them a word from God: he tells the people that they should not go to Egypt, but that they should, instead, stay where they are.

Despite their seemingly sincere request of Jeremiah, it turns out that the leaders had already made their own plan to go to Egypt. Even while they appeared to be waiting for guidance from God, they were busy making their plans, packing, and dreaming about their future in Egypt. They were certain that God would agree with what they had already planned to do—and they were unwilling to change their plans when God led them in a different direction.

What's more, the people fully expected that God would bless them . . . even if they disobediently went their own way.

If we read a little further in the book of Jeremiah, we discover that the people went forward with their own plan. They traveled to Egypt, and (of course) they encountered disastrous consequences.

When God gives us guidance—or when God reshapes plans that we have already made—we are wise to follow His counsel. Thankfully, God often redeems our disobedience. But how much better it is to follow His guidance in the first place.

There is no reason to suffer needless pain—and there is no reason to miss divine appointments—simply because we insist on going our own way.

God, sometimes it is hard for us to wait for Your direction. Instead of waiting, we are often inclined to come up with our own plan. We do pray about it. But what we often pray is that You would bless what we have already come up with. It is pretty easy for us to believe that You will bless something that we are already committed to . . . mostly because it is really hard for us to change direction at that point.

We realize, of course, how wrong this approach is. Still, it is going to be terribly hard for us to wait for You to speak. And it will be even harder for us simply to do what You tell us to do. Even so, help us to not pretend to want Your guidance—when what we really want is Your affirmation of our plans. Our plans are a sorry substitute for Your will. And what we want—what we truly want—is Your will.

Day 81

FREEDOM

*For freedom, Christ set us free. Stand firm then
and don't submit again to a yoke of slavery.*

GALATIANS 5:1

Many followers of Jesus who live in the Western world
associate "freedom" with "political freedom." When we
encounter biblical teaching about freedom, we often assume that we
are truly free only if we live in a country that allows us to live out our
faith freely. It is easy to make that assumption—especially if political
freedom is all that we have ever known.

Many of us have been blessed with political freedom—and it is
a wonderful gift to be able to worship freely, to be able to share our
faith freely, and to be able to live out our love for Jesus in bold and
public ways. That is a wonderful privilege that, of course, carries great
responsibility as well.

Surprisingly, that kind of freedom is not what the Bible is talking about when it talks about freedom. The kind of spiritual freedom
that is offered by Jesus is a freedom that is available to *every follower of
Jesus* regardless of where those followers might live. To put it plainly,
a follower of Jesus in North Korea is just as free as a follower in South
Carolina. A follower of Jesus in Iran is just as free as a believer in
Canada. As Paul makes clear in Galatians 5:1, Christ has liberated us
. . . to be free. And that freedom is a present reality for every follower
of Jesus.

Now, clearly, there may be different consequences as followers of Jesus in different places live out their faith. A believer in America, for example, might not pay a high price for attending a worship service. In America, we will not be arrested or harassed for participating in a Bible study or for sharing Jesus with a neighbor. A believer in North Korea will pay a significant price for doing those same things. But the believer in North Korea is just as free to obey Jesus as any believer anywhere.

Jesus has set His followers free. By His determination, we are free to be obedient. Followers of Jesus are *always* free to be obedient. In every circumstance and in every setting, followers of Jesus are free to obey Him.

Yes, of course—we can be punished by those in authority for obeying Jesus, but that punishment can never determine whether or not we will obey. The world can never take away what Jesus has granted. And Jesus has declared that we are free.

Consider once again the powerful stories that we have encountered in this book. Believers in persecution all around the world have decided—repeatedly—that they will obey Jesus even when there is a great cost. Jesus has set them free to obey—and they have decided that nothing will get in the way of their obedience.

It is fine to be thankful for our political freedom. But that political freedom—as wonderful as it is—is small compared to the spiritual freedom that Jesus has given us.

We have been set free. And because that is true, nothing should be able to stop us from obeying Jesus . . . even when obedience carries a high cost.

God, first, we acknowledge the simple fact that we have spiritual brothers and sisters in places like North Korea and Iran. That, in itself, is quite a surprise.

The next surprise is that those brothers and sisters who live in harsh and repressive environments are, by Your declaration, absolutely free to obey Jesus. Forgive us for our small thinking that suggests that punishment can keep someone from obeying You. In fact, You have set us free. At least part of what that means is that we are free to obey You.

Teach us that we are always free to obey You. Teach us that we are free to sacrifice. Teach us that we are free to lay down our lives.

We are, indeed, thankful for the political freedom that we enjoy. But, Lord, we are committed to serve and obey You with or without that kind of freedom.

Day 82

BEING ONE

"I have given them the glory that you have given me, so that
they may be one as we are one. I am in them and you are in me,
so that they may be completely one, that the world may know
you have sent me and have loved them as you have loved me."

JOHN 17:22–23

In this book, we have talked often about how crucial it is that we love the people of the world. That is a central command of the gospel and we take that command seriously. God loves the world—and it is our privilege to love the world that God loves.

In addition, it is crucial that we love our brothers and sisters in Christ.

In praying for those who would follow Him, Jesus prayed for unity. He suggested that the unity of His followers would demonstrate His presence and His power. This command to love the Christian family sounds simple, of course—but that is not always easily done. And it is not always done well.

When we first began our overseas service, we were not all that interested in working with followers of Jesus who were not a part of "our group." We are embarrassed to admit this—and we confess now that our attitude was small and limiting. We were not the only ones to do this, of course. Our sending agency was large and strong; we had so many resources that it sometimes seemed that we did not really need the help of anyone else. In addition, there were often doctrinal differences that made cooperation difficult. It was easy to draw lines and make boundaries; many of us were quite good at determining who was "in" and who was "out."

Admittedly, lines and boundaries can sometimes be helpful and necessary. But, in our case, our hesitance to work with other followers of Jesus sometimes damaged our witness. It was hard for others to see the unity that Jesus talked about. And without the gifts, resources, and leadership of other followers of Jesus, we were not able to do all that we could have done.

As time passed, we began to talk with followers of Jesus from other backgrounds and traditions. We began to listen and walk together. We discovered that many of these people loved Jesus as much as we did. We discovered that their hearts were broken for the world just as our hearts were. And we were delighted to see that our work could be multiplied when we worked together.

Especially when we faced crushing humanitarian needs, we learned quickly that we needed all the help we could get. Working together with other followers of Jesus, we were able to serve much more effectively. What's more, we were able to live out in the presence of the world the kind of unity that Jesus called us to embrace.

It sounds a little silly, but we discovered that many followers of Jesus from other backgrounds and traditions were just as committed to the Great Commission as we were. And whenever we were able to work together for a common purpose, we did just that.

It seems like a small thing, but our love for other believers communicates powerfully to the people we are seeking to serve.

Make us one, Lord Jesus. Even though we are different in many ways, make us one. In our willingness to love one another and work together, help us demonstrate that You have sent us and that You are empowering what we do.

Give us wisdom as we seek to serve You in the best possible way. Forgive us when we draw lines and establish boundaries when that is not necessary. Set us free to trust You and to share the work with all who belong to You.

ALWAYS PRESENT

Then he said, "Go out and stand on the mountain in the LORD's
presence." At that moment, the LORD passed by. A great and
mighty wind was tearing at the mountains and was shattering
cliffs before the LORD, the LORD was not in the wind. After
the wind there was an earthquake, but the LORD was not in
the earthquake. After the earthquake there was a fire, but the
LORD was not in the fire. And after the fire there was a voice,
a soft whisper. When Elijah heard it, he wrapped his face in his
mantle and went out and stood at the entrance of the cave.

1 KINGS 19:11–13A

Over the past few years, we have talked with followers of Jesus who have endured harsh and debilitating punishment. It is hard to imagine or describe the brutality of the torture, imprisonment, psychological torment, and humiliation that these believers have suffered. What might be worse than all of that, however, is the isolation and loneliness of their ordeals. Repeatedly, our persecuted friends talked about being separated from their beloved family members, being cut off from the church, and being unable to have any connection with their faith community as they suffered.

These same believers claimed that they were never truly alone.

Even in situations of complete isolation, these persecuted friends were always aware of the presence of God. They sensed that God was with them and they were confident that He would never leave. For many, this was the anchor that kept them alive. For many, this was the rock that provided their foundation. They discovered that God is faithful and always with His children.

Always!

In 1 Kings 19, we read about Elijah. After what we might call "a mountaintop experience" on Mount Carmel, Elijah is now running for his life. King Ahab has threatened him—and that threat sends Elijah into hiding.

While Elijah might be able to hide from King Ahab, he can never hide from God.

In truth, God can find us wherever we are. He promises never to leave us—and it is crucial that we remember and cling to that promise.

Even if we happen to be running away from God, God will still find His way to us.

British poet Francis Thompson wrote a book entitled *The Hound of Heaven*—a book based on the fact that God relentlessly pursues us. Even if we try to run away from God, Thompson says that we cannot outrun "those strong feet that follow . . . with unhurrying chase and unperturbed pace." Thompson's personal experience convinced him that God would never leave him—even if occasionally he wanted to get away from God. God, according to Thompson, is the hound of heaven!

Whether we are in prisons that others have forced us in—or in prisons that we have made ourselves—God is present. That is good news for us—and that is good news for a world filled with people who are lonely, broken, and (in some cases) actually running away from God.

Even in our isolation, we are never alone. God is *always* with us!

Faithful God, You are always with us. Where can we go to flee from You? Even if we try to escape You, You are present with us. In the darkest places, You are with us. When we fail, You are with us. When others do us harm, You are with us.

We are embarrassed to admit it, but we do sometimes try to escape You. Sometimes, we try to avoid Your call. But You pursue us relentlessly for our own good.

We long for Your embrace. We know that, without Your presence, we are lost. And we realize that You pursue every person on this planet the very same way that You pursue us. So we are, once again, drawn back to Your passion for the whole world. We are drawn back to our part in telling the world the story of Your love. We dare not keep the gift of Your presence to ourselves. We gladly share it with a broken world—this unbelievable news that "God is with us!" We gladly share this good news especially with people who are running away from You.

SEEKING SOMETHING

*"You will seek me and find me when you
search for me with all your heart."*

JEREMIAH 29:13

✝ The Ethiopian city of Harar is about five hundred kilometers east of Addis Ababa. On the list of cities sacred to Islam, Harar is number four. It follows Mecca, Medina, and Jerusalem. Within the walls of the ancient center of the city, there are ninety-nine mosques.

Several years ago, we were in Harar a day or two before the end of Ramadan. The city was crammed with people preparing Eid, the celebration that ends the annual month of fasting. The crowd was so thick that it was almost impossible to move through the narrow streets. People were shopping for food, for gifts, and for special items for the upcoming celebration.

It seemed as if the entire world was there. And everyone, it seemed, was looking for something.

That phrase accurately describes every person in our world; we are all looking for something. We simply cannot help ourselves. We may not even be able to identify what it is that we're seeking, but we are all on a mission to find . . . to find what exactly?

We are desperate to find our Creator, to find our purpose, to find a calling, to find a place to belong, to find forgiveness, to find rescue, to find life.

Scripture makes it clear that, ultimately, it is God who finds us. Still, we cannot stop our seeking. That is simply how God has made us. We are seekers. And we cannot rest until we find what it is that we were meant to find.

Jeremiah 29:13 reminds us of our true nature and our character as human beings. By design, God has made us to be seekers. Further, God assures us that, by His grace, we will be successful in our search. When we search with all our heart—when our search is honest and sincere—we will, in fact, be satisfied.

Ultimately, we are looking for God. And God Himself tells us that He will allow Himself to be found!

That is a wonderful word of grace, a delightful promise of assurance. In a world filled with passionate seekers, God will allow Himself to be found.

That day in Harar, everyone seemed to be looking for something. Some of those people might even have been looking for God. If so, God assures us that such a search will bear fruit.

In His grace, God rewards honest seekers.

God, we celebrate the fact that You allow Yourself to be found. As we think about our story with You, we identify seasons in our lives that were truly seasons of seeking. And then we identify wonderful moments when our seeking led us to You. Thank You for Your grace revealed so beautifully in Your allowing Yourself to be found.

Even as we thank You for that, however, we realize that many people in this world are still seeking. They may not even know

*that they are looking for You, but we understand that You
are the ultimate desire of every search. Empower us to assist
those who search. Give us words to speak and deeds to share
so that others might see You and find You and know You.*

*We pray that all who sincerely seek You will
come to know Your great love.*

Day 85

A GLIMPSE OF HEAVEN

> *Then I saw another angel flying high overhead, with the*
> *eternal gospel to announce to the inhabitants of the earth—*
> *to every nation, tribe, language, and people. He spoke with*
> *a loud voice: "Fear God and give him glory, because the*
> *hour of his judgment has come. Worship the one who made*
> *heaven and earth, the sea and the springs of water."*
>
> REVELATION 14:6–7

In many great cities of the world, we have found churches where people from many different languages and nations gather to worship. Sometimes these churches can be found even in cities where there is significant persecution and clear pressure *not* to be a follower of Jesus. Even so, there are communities that are called "international churches." The presence of these churches has sometimes surprised us.

In one large African city, we attended a worship service at a large international church. The service was simple and clearly designed to honor God. The message was explicitly evangelistic and quite encouraging. We sang songs that were meaningful and moving. We celebrated the Lord's Supper.

But what stood out to us, more than anything, was the makeup of the congregation.

While we worshipped, we thought of the words of Psalm 86:9.

All the nations you have made will come and bow down
before you, Lord, and will honor your name.

The word *international* in the name of the church is not an accident. Sitting in the balcony, we looked down upon six or seven hundred people representing dozens and dozens of different people groups. Some people there that day were dressed in national garb and were easy to identify. Some people were singing the congregational songs in languages other than English. Some people proudly mentioned their country of origin during the greeting time. The diversity of the gathered group was apparent at every turn.

On the Sunday we were there, the worship leaders took time to acknowledge every country that was represented. They first asked everyone to stand. Then they warmly greeted the people from their home country and had those people sit down. Then they greeted the people from the United States and Canada—and had those people sit down. Then the leaders moved throughout the sanctuary and asked each person still standing to identify his or her country. Eventually, every country represented in that room was named.

On the day we were there, more than sixty countries were named. And some of those names included places that we considered "unlikely" places to find followers of Jesus. Sadly, it is easy for us to assume that certain people in certain places are beyond the reach of God's grace. But as Psalm 86:9 reminds us, *all* (not *many*, but *all*!) the nations God has made will one day worship Him.

Obviously, not every nation in the world was represented in the worship service that day. But many were! And celebrating the richness and diversity of that gathered group, we sensed that we were catching a glimpse of what heaven will look like one day.

The real miracle is not that all those other people get to be included. The real miracle . . . is that we are included!

God of the Nations, thank You for reminding us that Your grace is offered to everyone! Thank You for reminding us that no one is beyond Your reach. Thank You for reminding us that no place is off-limits to Your gracious activity.

Give us eyes that see the world the way You see the world. Help us to see people—all people—the way You see people. Give us a heart for the world—even as we celebrate the wonder of being included in Your family ourselves.

Day 86

DECEPTIVE FINALITY

> *When it was already evening, because it was the day of*
> *preparation (that is, the day before the Sabbath), Joseph of*
> *Arimathea, a prominent member of the Sanhedrin who was*
> *himself looking forward to the kingdom of God, came and*
> *boldly went to Pilate and asked for Jesus's body. Pilate was*
> *surprised that he was already dead. Summoning the centurion,*
> *he asked him whether he had already died. When he found*
> *out from the centurion, he gave the corpse to Joseph. After he*
> *bought some linen cloth, Joseph took him down and wrapped*
> *him in the linen. Then he laid him in a tomb cut out of the*
> *rock and rolled a stone against the entrance to the tomb.*

MARK 15:42–46

One of the most troubling parts of the gospel story is how fast things change from Sunday to Friday during the days leading up to Jesus' crucifixion. On Sunday of that week, Jesus makes His way into Jerusalem among cheering and adoring crowds. He is celebrated as a hero. He is welcomed as a friend. Today, we call that day "Palm Sunday." In a matter of days, however, there is a dramatic turn. The cheering is replaced by jeering. The crowds that cry out their adoration quickly give way to crowds that call for crucifixion.

By the end of the week, Jesus is dead. If we were to put a title on Mark 15:42–46, we might call this part of the story, "It Sure Looks Like It's Over to Me."

Some scholars are critical of Joseph of Arimathea. They say that he should have spoken up sooner and that he should have done something before Jesus' death. On the other hand, his behavior at this point in the story is remarkably courageous. He is one of the Jewish leaders—and he stands as evidence that not *all* of the Jewish leaders wanted Jesus to be put to death. Joseph went boldly to Pilate and dared to ask for Jesus' body. His request was granted. Joseph prepared Jesus' body for burial and then placed the body in a cave-like tomb. He then rolled a stone against the entrance of the tomb.

There is nothing like a burial to tell us that the story is over.

Very early on Easter morning in 1997, our sixteen-year-old son died in Nairobi soon after being rushed to the hospital. His name was Tim. Tim was an amazing young man—loved by all who knew him, joyful and hopeful, deeply in love with Jesus. Decades later, we cannot put into words the depth of our sorrow and heartache when Tim died. It is sorrow and heartache that we still carry today.

About a week or so after Tim's death, hundreds of people gathered for Tim's memorial service in an outdoor amphitheater at the school where Tim had been a high school sophomore. Rain started to fall just as the service came to an end. At the conclusion of the service, the crowd walked down the hill to the place where Tim would be buried, right there on the school campus.

Here is what Ruth's brother wrote about what happened next:

> *After we prayed and sang down there at the bottom of the hill, Nik and Ruth led about six hundred people back up the hill for a time of fellowship and reception. For some reason, I stayed there at the graveside. There were about twelve of us who stayed there, the others were Kenyan workers and*

helpers who were also friends of Nik and Ruth. I felt that I was representing the family. Nik and Ruth, I am sure, knew what was about to happen, but I was completely unaware of Kenyan tradition. Nik and Ruth had to be back at the school with the people, but I was able to stay by the graveside.

In just a few moments, I realized what was about to happen. I will never forget the instant it dawned on me that we were going to bury Tim.

The casket was lowered into the grave—with just ropes and hands—and then four people picked up shovels and began filling the grave. When they were tired, others took their places. I found myself doing what everybody else was doing. Shovels were passed around. Sometimes people simply used their hands. The rain, the tears, the sweat; who could tell the difference? Sometimes we worked in silence. Sometimes there was a story or two. Sometimes somebody sang a few lines of a song. Sometimes there was even laughter. Sometimes there were wails of grief. Red, wet, Kenyan mud was everywhere. And together, we literally buried Tim.

There was no stone covering the entrance to the tomb, but we did exactly what Joseph of Arimathea did.

There is nothing quite like a burial to tell us that the story is over. Except . . . the burial is not the end.

The truth of this story—and the truth of every good burial—is that the finality is a deception. The story is not over at all! No stone is ever the last act when it is rolled up against something in which God has a part. And that is true not just about death. There are so many things we are inclined to put away. "Well, that's the end of that!" we say. "That's the end of that chapter! That's the end of that story. It's over."

But God does not pay attention to our finalities.

God has so many ways of opening up things that are sealed up tight. And the fact that He can do that with Jesus and His tomb . . . means that He can do that with Tim . . . and it means that He can do that with you too.

And the fact that God can do that with death means that He can do that with all of our other finalities as well. All of those places where we have decided that God is not going to work. All of those people we have labeled as beyond God's power to reach. All of those relationships we have written off. All of those people groups who are beyond hope.

We simply must understand this: we think we know what the finalities are . . . but God barely notices.

There is nothing like a burial to tell us that the story is over.

Except . . . the story is not over at all.

Life-giving, death-defying God, forgive us for saying that the story is over. We look at our world and we see only impossibility. We obviously know when something is over. We know when it is time to give up hope. We know what a burial means.

But You shake Your head at our foolish pronouncements. You tell us quietly that You hold every story in Your hands. You assure us that no story is finished until You say that it is finished. Forgive us for giving up. Forgive us for walking away. Forgive us for deciding exactly where You can work—and where You cannot work. Forgive us for declaring that certain people are beyond Your reach.

Indeed, You are the God who gives life and defies death. Despite our convictions about finalities, we will wait and we will allow You to have the last word.

SELFISH WITH THE GIFT

"Then everyone who calls on the name of the Lord will be saved."
ACTS 2:21

When Tim died, we were surrounded and embraced by the community of faith. Because we were so far from home, our own families were not able to be present. But God provided a family in Kenya to love us and care for us in that time of profound grief. Beloved people from Tim's school, from our mission community, from our church in Kenya, and from our neighborhood flocked to our home to meet every possible need. The presence of these dear people saved our lives.

One night that week, while we were meeting to plan Tim's memorial service, there was a knock on the door. When we opened the door, we were amazed to see one of our staff workers from Somalia. He was a Muslim man who had completed a treacherous journey of five days to be with us in Nairobi. He had walked through the desert, hitchhiked, ridden in the back of trucks, crossed rivers, and somehow navigated a border crossing (a passage that was probably illegal at the time).

He knocked on our door to say that he had come "to bury *our* son Tim."

In using the word "our," this dear Muslim friend was saying that, because of his love for us, he considered Tim to be his son too.

At the memorial service, our friend sat with us in the front row. He heard the story of Jesus clearly. He heard words of deep grief and words of certain hope. He heard beautiful music that gave glory to God for His love and care. He heard about the promise of eternal life and he heard about the possibility of forgiveness. It was obvious that our friend was deeply touched and profoundly moved. The gathered community embraced him as a family member.

Some time later in Mogadishu, he talked with us and the Somali staff about the memorial service and about all that he had witnessed. Clearly, he had understood the words and the meaning of what had been shared. And he was thrilled with what he had experienced. But the question he asked us stopped us in our tracks:

> *"Why,"* he said, *"have followers of Jesus kept Jesus to themselves? Why have my people not heard this before now? Why have followers of Jesus not shared Jesus with us?"*

We didn't know what to say, nor could we anticipate the reaction from our Muslim staff members. As excited as we were by his positive response to what he had heard during the funeral about Jesus, we were devastated by this question. Even though we had worked with this friend for years—and even though we had shared the story of Jesus with him and other staff members many times—he had apparently never heard the gospel with this kind of clarity.

Even more, he was aware that millions of his people had never heard the gospel in any way at all.

This is the question that should keep us up at night. This is the question that should inform our prayers. This is the question that should affect every single thing we do. And this is the question that should cause us to change. This is the question that should cause *every follower of Jesus* to change: *Why would we ever keep Jesus to ourselves? Why would we choose not to share Jesus with every person in this world? Why would we not do that . . . today?*

Lord, forgive us.

The question is a haunting question, a convicting question. And we have no excuse. It is never our intention, of course, to keep Jesus to ourselves. But, in fact, we do exactly that far too often. We keep Jesus to ourselves when we refuse to share, when we fail to embrace Your call, when we are blind to opportunity, when we walk away because the required sacrifice is simply too great.

Lord, forgive us.

Lord, forgive us—and, then, change us. Help us to make different decisions. Help us to embrace risk. Help us to be different.

Lord, help us to never again keep Jesus to ourselves.

Day 88

Victorious Suffering

He was despised and rejected by men, a man of suffering
who knew what sickness was. He was like someone people
turned away from; he was despised, and we didn't value
him. Yet he himself bore our sicknesses, and he carried our
pains; but we in turn regarded him stricken, struck down
by God, and afflicted. But he was pierced because of our
rebellion, crushed because of our iniquities; punishment for
our peace was on him, and we are healed by his wounds.

Isaiah 53:3–5

Isaiah 52:13–53:12 is one of the so-called Servant Songs. If we ever needed to be reminded that God's ways are not our ways, this Servant Song makes the point very strongly.

This passage is one of the best-known passages in all the Old Testament. Almost every verse in Isaiah 52:13–53:12 is quoted somewhere in the New Testament. This is a remarkable section of Scripture that points squarely to the death—and to the resurrection—of Christ. Some people consider these verses to be the very heart of Old Testament Scripture.

Beyond all of that, this passage is a startling reminder of God's unusual ways. We are reminded here that God has a radically different perspective. The world says one thing—but God says something else. The world reaches one conclusion—but God comes to a different assessment. The world is disappointed that things didn't turn out better—but God claims that everything has turned out just right. That is the message of this Servant Song.

Consider the middle part of this Servant Song (Isaiah 53:1–9). This is what some people say about God's chosen Servant. This is what the world sees. In these verses, we find a report about a terrible event—an event that the world considers a failure, a tragedy, a disaster. The theme of this middle section of the Servant Song is *suffering*. The Servant is described here as a man of sorrows.

But that is not all that this Servant Song is about. The beginning of the passage (Isa. 52:13–15) and the closing of the passage (Isa. 53:10–12) reveal the true focus of the story. And the true focus of the story is not on the suffering, but on the victory. The middle section of the song reflects the view of the world—while the beginning and ending of the song give us the perspective of God.

And what exactly does God say about all this? Well, God certainly sees the suffering—but God sees something else as well.

Consider God's point of view.

The world is offended by the Servant's suffering. The world cannot even bear to look at the Servant. The world is horrified by His physical appearance. But this is all part of God's plan. This is all God's will. This is precisely how God has chosen to deal with sin. If we read Isaiah 52:13–15 and Isaiah 53:10–12 carefully, we are stunned into silence by God's unusual ways.

Several times in this book, we have talked about the erroneous view that if we do what is right, God will surely protect us and keep us safe. We want so much to believe that faithfulness will always result in blessing (and we will typically go even further and claim that we truly know what "blessing" is).

But if that is the truth, then Jesus would never have ended up on the cross. In the nick of time, the Father would have intervened and rescued Him. Before Jesus' death, the Father would have stepped in and He would have said, "No you don't! This is My Son! Leave Him alone!"

But that is not what happened.

Could it be that Jesus' suffering was specifically part of God's plan? Could it be that Jesus' suffering was a *necessary* part of God's plan? Could it be that the cross was not some terrible accident—but something that, by God's determination, simply had to happen? Could it be that it was the Lord's will "to crush him severely" (Isa. 53:10)?

And could it be that the suffering of followers of Jesus is part of God's plan as well? Could it be that *your* suffering is part of God's plan?

A central theme of this section of Isaiah—and a central theme of all of Scripture—is that this suffering Servant will gain victory in the end. This is ultimately a story of triumph. But He will gain victory not *in spite of the suffering—but because of it!*

And that is a crucial word for those of us who desire to avoid suffering at all costs. Much to our amazement, sometimes the suffering is exactly what God has in mind. And we can live with that because we know—without any doubt!—that God knows exactly what He is doing. We can live with that because we know—without any doubt!— that this is ultimately a story of victory.

We have been reading about profound suffering—grappling with the certainty of sacrifice in our lives. At this point, we might be wondering what all those persecuted brothers and sisters in Christ did to deserve such pain. We might pridefully wonder if perhaps they were not being faithful—and that perhaps their suffering was punishment for their unfaithfulness. We might even pat ourselves on the back and feel that we have somehow done something right to avoid that kind of suffering.

If we happen to think those things—we should consider this startling possibility: could it be that our suffering brothers and sisters in Christ have experienced such horrible persecution *because of* their faithfulness?

Persecuted followers of Jesus will likely understand the perspective of God much better than we do. And they will likely read Isaiah 52:13–53:12 with very different eyes.

Yes, God will have His way. Yes, God will win in the end. But God will use Jesus' suffering—and God will use our suffering as well—to gain His victory. God will use suffering to redeem this broken world.

Ultimately, God will have His way not in spite of suffering, but because of it.

God, we love to talk about victory. But we are sobered by the path that You set before Your people. Yes, that path leads to victory—but that path goes directly through the valley of suffering. We realize that we can add nothing to what Jesus has done, but we also know that we are called to share in His sufferings. We do not understand why it should be that way.

More to the point, we do not understand You.

Even so, we are committed to You. We submit to You. You are our Lord. And that means that if our suffering is part of Your plan, then we will embrace that suffering. We will embrace that suffering for Your glory and for our good.

Lord God, Your ways are not our ways. Our thoughts are not Your thoughts. But You are God and we are not.

Day 89

SACRIFICING OUR SUPPOSED SECURITY

> *The entire Israelite community departed from Elim and*
> *came to the Wilderness of Sin, which is between Elim and*
> *Sinai, on the fifteenth day of the second month after they*
> *had left the land of Egypt. The entire Israelite community*
> *grumbled against Moses and Aaron in the wilderness. The*
> *Israelites said to them, "If only we had died by the LORD's*
> *hand in the land of Egypt, when we sat by pots of meat and*
> *ate all the bread we wanted. Instead, you brought us into*
> *this wilderness to make this whole assembly die of hunger!"*
>
> EXODUS 16:1–3

In a dramatic way, God had rescued His people and set them free. Enslaved in Egypt, without any real hope of anything ever being different, God had stepped in and brought about a miraculous change. The people had seen, with their own eyes, that God was able. God had not only brought them out of Egypt, but he had brought them through the Red Sea.

Amazingly, God had set His people free.

But this freedom had an odd look—at least at this point in the story. At this point in the story, freedom looked like . . . wilderness. Freedom looked uncertain. Freedom looked dangerous.

And all of a sudden, a frightening thought crossed the minds of these wide-eyed pilgrims: *is freedom something we really want?* This life of freedom was so difficult, in fact, that they began to think fondly of Egypt. They began to think about how things used to be.

Granted, life was not perfect in Egypt. The people had to work hard and the conditions were brutal, but there was a measure of safety in Egypt. There was a measure of security in Egypt. It was not a great life, but at least it was a *known* life.

And looking back, the people remembered life in Egypt to be better than it really was.

The people honestly began to wonder if what they had in Egypt was better than this "freedom" that God had given them. *We were secure back in Egypt, they thought. And this new freedom that we have now feels downright scary. Egypt was not really all that bad, was it?*

Of course, their memories of Egypt were distorted. Deeply distorted. They dreamed about "the good old days" that really were not good at all. But here in the wilderness—in this terribly insecure setting—distorted memories began to take center stage. "Don't you remember how good it was back in Egypt?" the people said to one another (16:3). "Back in Egypt, we ate all the food we wanted."

We find the same distorted memories in Numbers 11:5: "We remember the free fish we ate in Egypt, along with the cucumbers, melons, leeks, onions, and garlic."

But we cannot get any of that out here in the wilderness . . .

There are a couple of problems with this kind of remembering.

First, it is simply not honest. This kind of remembering is distorted. It calls to mind a time in Egypt that never really existed. It ignores the brutal reality of the way life actually was back in Egypt.

The second problem is even more serious. The ancient Hebrews were dreaming about a kind of security that does not really exist. It did not exist back in Egypt; it simply does not exist anywhere in this life. The Israelites wanted so much to know how things would be for them; they wanted to know what would happen next; they wanted to know that everything would turn out fine. But they simply could not know those things—either in Egypt or out here in the wilderness.

In fact, we can never know those things.

Security is an idol. It is an idol that holds remarkable power over human beings, but it is an idol nonetheless.

And unless we guard against it, this is how we will begin to think: *It is too risky to serve God. It is too risky to make sacrifices. It is too risky to go out on mission. It is too risky to take our children with us overseas. It is too risky to get involved in the lives of other people. It is too risky to be generous with our resources. It is too risky to share our faith. It is too risky to trust God with our future.*

And that kind of thinking leads us to the ultimate question:

Will we stay in Egypt? Or will we follow the call of God?

That is surely the question of the book of Exodus, but that is also the question that we deal with every day. On the one hand, there is the idol of security (distorted though it may be). On the other hand, there is the adventure (and the very real danger!) of walking obediently with God.

If we look back and remember our lives before we began this grand adventure of walking with Jesus—and if those memories cause us to think that life back then was something wonderful—then our memories are not honest. As dangerous as this adventure with Jesus may be, we would never consider exchanging this adventure for the life we had before we started walking with Jesus. We need honest memories: life was miserable back in Egypt—and there is no way in the world that we would ever choose that life over the one we have now.

We were made for this risky pilgrimage with this God who can rescue His people and part the Red Sea and provide manna in the wilderness. We were made for this holy adventure.

And we will never be whole until we embrace all that Jesus has in store for us.

God would never dream of allowing us to settle for the idol of security when there is abundant life to be found in this journey of trust and obedience.

Do we really want to go back to Egypt?

Our memories are playing tricks on us. That life that we knew before this adventure began was not nearly as good as we think it was. And, honestly, it was not secure at all. Why would we ever settle for that—when we can actually walk with God here and now?

There is no future in Egypt. The only future is found on pilgrimage with this great and glorious God. This God who knows exactly what He is doing. This God who is going somewhere. This God who is able to accomplish His purposes. This God who knows that the only true security can be found in Him.

This is an easy choice. The people of God *always* choose to journey with God.

Always.

Lord God, we choose You. Egypt calls to us. We think of earlier days and we think that those earlier days were better, safer, more secure, more predictable. But our minds are playing tricks on us. Even though life with You—now— seems dangerous and risky and unpredictable, we would not trade what we have with You now for anything!

What a joy to be on journey with You! What a joy to be part of this holy adventure! We refuse to bow down to the idol of security. We place our lives in Your hands. And if You call us to hard places, if You call us into the wilderness, if You call us into the unknown, that is exactly where we want to be.

Quite simply, we want to be with You.

Lord God, we choose You.

Day 90

YOUR STORY

"Choose for yourselves today: Which will you worship . . . ?"
JOSHUA 24:15B

 So what comes next?

It is not enough simply to read about persecuted followers of Jesus in other parts of the world. It is not enough to be moved by their faith and commitment. It is not even enough to thank God for those faithful brothers and sisters and to pray for them as they deal with suffering and oppression.

It is not enough to encounter great truths in Scripture and to absorb those truths. It is not enough to marvel at the activity of God and to believe that God is doing today what He has always done.

It is not enough to ask yourself challenging questions and evaluate how you are doing. It is not enough even to make commitments and decisions about how you will be different moving forward.

As wonderful as it is, it is not even enough simply to pray—even if our prayers are sincere and heartfelt.

We might do well to choose to do all of those things—but what remains is our action. What remains is our response.

Will we, in fact, go across the street? Will we cross the ocean? Will we share Jesus with the people in our own home? Will we pour ourselves into our churches and small groups and live out this adventure of faithfulness that is ours to embrace?

Will we choose a life of sacrifice so that others might have an opportunity to know Jesus?

Will we share generously the money that God has placed in our hands? Will our time belong to Him? Will we risk embarrassment, inconvenience, and even ridicule to live out our faith? Will we be willing to change?

Might we even be willing to take up a cross—and lay down our lives?

In a sense, time will reveal exactly what we will do.

But it will not take a long time for that to be revealed. In all likelihood, what we do in the next few hours or in the next couple of days will reveal how deeply we have been seized by this call of God . . . to sacrifice our very selves for the sake of the gospel.

And we will be able to measure if our hearts truly belong to Him by our willingness . . . to walk across the street . . . or cross the ocean . . . so that others might hear about Jesus.

Almighty God, what we do next will reveal what we believe about You. What we do next will reveal what we believe about Your call. What we do next will reveal if reading this devotional book has been merely interesting—or if it has helped us love You more completely.

Break our hearts for this broken world. Empower us to share, to give, to pray, to serve, to help, to go.

Empower us to sacrifice for the sake of Your kingdom.

NOTES

1. Oswald Chambers, *The Complete Works of Oswald Chambers* (Grand Rapids: Discovery House Publishers, 2000), 832. From *My Utmost for His Highest*; entry for October 11.

2. Dietrich Bonhoeffer, *The Cost of Discipleship* (New York: Macmillan, rev. ed., 1999), 99.

3. In *The Insanity of God*, we used the name Tavian for security reasons. Now that Constantine is with his Lord, we want to honor him by using his real name.

4. Oswald Chambers, *The Complete Works of Oswald Chambers* (Grand Rapids: Discovery House Publishers, 2000), 795. From *My Utmost for His Highest*, June 28.

Also by
NIK RIPKEN

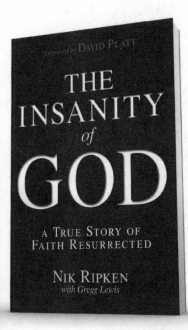

THE WORLDWIDE BESTSELLER

"This is a book that every well-meaning Christian ought to read. It gives the most comprehensive overview of what life is like for the true followers of Jesus who are willing to pay the whole price for following Him. Extremely touching at times. It makes you cry and it makes you laugh. But remember they are your brothers and mine. Therefore we have a responsibility of standing with them as part of the body of Christ worldwide."

- BROTHER ANDREW
Founder, Open Doors International,
Author, *God's Smuggler and Secret Believers*

The Insanity of God tells a story—a remarkable and unique story to be sure, yet at heart a very human story—of the Ripkens' own spiritual and emotional odyssey. The gripping, narrative account of a personal pilgrimage into some of the toughest places on earth, combined with sobering and insightful stories of the remarkable people of faith Nik and Ruth encountered on their journeys, will serve as a powerful course of revelation, growth, and challenge for anyone who wants to know whether God truly is enough.

Also by
NIK RIPKEN

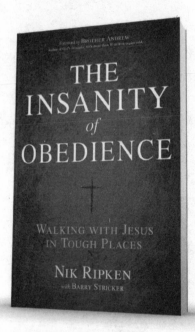

A CALL TO
PRACTICAL ACTION

The Insanity of Obedience is a bold challenge to global discipleship. Nik Ripken exposes the danger of safe Christianity and calls readers to something greater. The Insanity of Obedience challenges Christians in the same, provocative way that Jesus did. This book dares you—and prepares you—to cross the street and the oceans with the Good News of Jesus Christ.